THE ROOM

G000242785

Over 100 practical plans
for your home

THE ROOM PLANNER

Over 100 practical plans
for your home

Paula Robinson and Phil Robinson

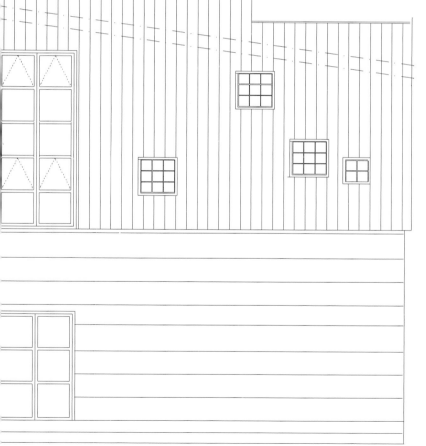

EBURY
PRESS

First published in Great Britain in 2005

1 3 5 7 9 10 8 6 4 2

Text and illustrations © Paula Robinson and Phil Robinson 2005

All the illustrations in this book are originated or adapted by Phil Robinson. We would like to express our thanks to the architects who permitted us to use their plans.

A CIP catalogue record for this book is available from the British Library.

Ebury Press
Random House,
20 Vauxhall Bridge Road,
London SW1V 2SA

Random House Australia (Pty) Limited
20 Alfred Street,
Milsons Point,
Sydney,
New South Wales 2061,
Australia

Random House New Zealand Limited
18 Poland Road,
Glenfield,
Auckland 10,
New Zealand

Random House (Pty) Limited
Endulini,
5a Jubilee Road,
Parktown 2193, South Africa

The Random House Group Limited Reg. No. 954009
www.randomhouse.co.uk

Editors: Margaret Gilbey and Ali Glenny

Design and illustrations: Phil Robinson

ISBN 0 0919 0174 X
Printed and bound in China by C&C Offset Printing Co., Ltd.

For Leon – and Livia

Contents

*P*urchasing a home brings with it a natural desire to personalize the living space. As a homeowner – or prospective homeowner – you need a home that caters to your individual needs and is a unique statement of who you are and what you aspire to. You will no doubt also want to create a nest egg: a property that will increase in value thanks to the thought, time and effort that have been invested in it.

Nowadays designing your ideal home and getting the most from your investment demands a little more thought and planning than in times gone by. Technological innovations and flexible working arrangements, for instance, are significantly affecting the layouts of homes. Incorporating technology into the fabric of the property is no longer viewed as a luxury, but as a necessity.

Our altering lifestyles mean that we are beginning to discard the idea of activity-specific rooms and instead are embracing freer, more versatile living spaces. Eventually we will be able to 'draw our walls' at will, just as we currently draw our curtains: spaces will transform from open-plan to cosy and intimate at the touch of a button. Investing in home improvements these days definitely means having an eye on the future when it comes to layout and technology.

While many owners call on the help of architects and designers to create their dream home, others want a more hands-on approach. But moulding a property to match one's dreams and practical aspirations can be daunting to say the very least. Where to begin?

The aim of this book is to provide an inspiring and practical guide to tackling the task of reconfiguring a property. In each chapter, we will first give you an overview of how our homes will change to meet our different needs and lifestyles. This should help you to make personal choices for your home that will see you through the long term. While it is impossible to cover every single issue, we will try to highlight some of the key ones that need to be considered and worked through.

We will then show you 'before' and 'after' plans and provide clear, easy-to-follow projects that demonstrate just some of the many possibilities for transforming properties into homes that cater for individual needs, without losing sight of the long term. Finally, whatever your living space, the Basics chapter at the end of the book will give you some helpful hints on what to look out for while planning your home.

We intend to give you food for thought, and a sense of how your home could be adapted to suit your personal tastes and lifestyle, while still being highly practical and maintaining its resale value for the future.

We hope to fire your imagination by introducing you to the world of possibilities just waiting to be discovered out there. If you read a chapter, look at the plans and then come up with an inspired solution of your own for your home, then this book has done its job.

A few words of caution: before launching into transforming your home after your 'Eureka!' moment, do remember to check your plans with a structural engineer or architect, and do consult your local authority regarding any building or planning regulations that may be in force where you live. Tackle the potential issues and red tape before they come and tackle you.

Before exploring the many possibilities for reshaping your property, it is important to get a sense of just how homes are likely to change in the future. Armed with this knowledge, you will be able to make decisions that will work for you not just today, but also for many years to come.

Looking ahead

Rooms are out, spaces are in

In the West, we tend to think of 'home' as a place divided into a number of function-specific rooms: living room, dining room, bedrooms, etc. This has been the 'norm' for over 600 years, ever since the Italian Renaissance revolutionized the layout of houses. But contemporary needs and ideals are forcing us to re-evaluate both our concept of our homes and our way of living in them. Our daily lives have always been very much place-related: we live in our homes, we go to the office, we meet up with friends within our community. For centuries we have been living within clearly defined, physical places.

Now globalization and the Internet have expanded those boundaries and introduced us to a notion of flow never before experienced. Our lives are no longer confined to places, but can expand into endless spaces through the information superhighway. To keep up with this high-speed way of living, our homes need to kiss the Renaissance goodbye and embrace the future.

SPACE DIVISIONS

Homes will become spaces that we alter at will. Within a fixed, outer perimeter, we will be able to open and close the internal spaces of our home to suit our personal requirements.

Historically, open-plan spaces have presented their own problems, such as ensuring adequate heating, insulation and ventilation within a space. But new technology has solved many such issues. With these under control, we have the freedom to choose how we live our lives. From blinds that drop out of their concealed ceiling positions, to solid walls that slide back completely into other walls; from movable glass walls that can be clear or opaque at the touch of a button, to fabric divisions that change colour to suit. Divisions of space can be – or appear to be – as permanent or impermanent as we desire.

SPACES CREATED BY OUR WHIMS

The layout of our homes will increasingly be guided by mood and practical considerations, not by the constraints of a home's original construction.

When entertaining requires a large open span of space, divisions can be retracted to allow free circulation in a home.

When a more cosy, secluded atmosphere is required, divisions can be reintroduced in a configuration to suit.

Individual preference will govern whether an area is large or small, with change only the touch of a few buttons away. Optical illusion will add some fun and fantasy to our new homes: what appears solid and unyielding – floor-to-ceiling pillars for example – will in fact be a lightweight element that can be reconfigured in an instant.

Keeping the noise down

Much thought and design planning are required to make our new homes work. Imagination and flexibility need to go hand in hand with practical considerations.

Sound insulation is vital for certain spaces, given the variety of personalities and activities that converge in most homes. Shutting out noise from bedrooms and home offices will always be essential and must be designed for. But technological advances mean that effective partitioning no longer needs to be cumbersome, obtrusive and unsightly.

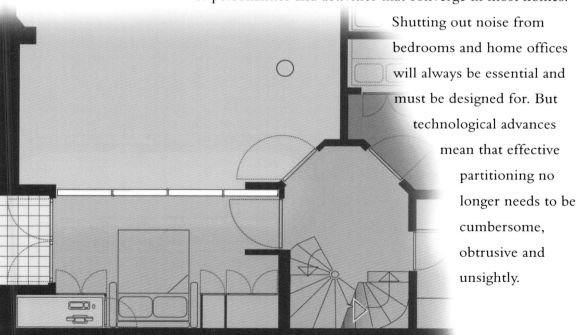

Problem solving with imagination

A space needs to work visually in all aspects, whether in open-plan mode, or in partitioned mode. To be a plausible chameleon, it can provide no clues to its other guises.

Floor covering is a big issue: our love of the softness and comfort of fitted carpeting is deep-rooted but fraught with problems. Carpet's flexible pile gives way under the weight of furniture and partitions, leaving tell-tale signs once pieces have been moved and walls retracted. Hard floor coverings – from wood to concrete – offer practicality and clean lines, but most of us still have a soft spot for comfort. However, while experience has taught us, for instance, that concrete is cold, hard and inflexible, it is now being presented to us in areas that we would normally expect to be warm and soft. With underfloor heating and a clear sealant, a concrete floor that is warm to the touch and smooth is a welcome shock.

The notion of 'expect the unexpected' in home design keeps us alert and receptive by pushing our boundaries beyond our in-built comfort zone. When change surprises us pleasantly, we are more inclined to welcome it with open arms.

Our old favourites put to new uses

The human fascination with both water and fire is as strong today as ever before. For centuries the Chinese have been using the soothing sound and relaxing flow of water to encourage energy flow in homes. In the West, fireplaces have been focal points, offering warmth, relaxation and comfort. We can look forward to some very unusual applications of both water and fire to enhance our homes.

WATER REDESIGNED

Where we were once content to see flowing water only in fish tanks and small water features, entire floor areas can now be given over to a view of flowing water underneath a transparent surface. At once both aesthetically pleasing and practical as underfloor heating, this concept appeals to our need for movement and change. It also allows great scope for lighting and colour variations to alter mood and atmosphere.

A water floor can easily adapt to the occupants' requirements: darkened and with no sound discernible when distractions would be intrusive during working time; illuminated to the intensity of light and to the colour required for when we are relaxing or entertaining. The principle is adaptable to both large and small scale, offering solid floor interspersed by clear, covered water channels as an alternative for those less inclined to 'walk on water'!

On the vertical plane, the serene effects of the water weir – a wall of softly flowing water – may start to play a more prominent role in our homes. An acknowledged method of counteracting noise in commercial settings, the water weir is a highly effective way of masking the clatter of conflicting activities in a busy household.

FIRE IS BACK

For centuries the fireplace was literally the heart of the home, and we are rediscovering the benefits of siting it in the centre of a space. Here it is a focal point for an open-plan space, but can still be part of any room division that we choose. This in turn enables us to look to new arrangements for our furnishings. Where the square and rectangular layout once dominated our living spaces – due both to the shapes of our rooms and to the location of fireplaces on walls – the circular or centrifugal layout is now coming into its own. The latter is more in keeping with our new lifestyles: easy and flowing, as opposed to regimented and angular.

Pro-active furniture

Spaces that adapt to individuals require flexibility in their furnishings. If retracting a wall entails bringing in a moving company and a design team to rearrange the furniture, this defeats the whole object of flexible space. Our furniture and product designers are having to re-evaluate design in relation to the people who use it. The all-important factors, beyond aesthetics, are comfort, ease of movement and maintenance.

With the ever-growing choice of materials, designers have ample opportunity to be lateral in their creations. They are enjoying challenging our concept of reality with furniture that appears impressive and unmovable, but can be pushed into new positions with ease.

Indulging our instincts

For many years our only concession to the changing seasons was in terms of clothing and perhaps food. Our daily routines and living spaces took no account of either seasonal cycles or our own physical and mental responses to them. There was a tendency to view everything as a continuum, with little or no awareness of diurnal, let alone seasonal, change.

Fortunately, we are now allowing ourselves to respond to our instincts. Different seasons and different times of the day beckon us into different areas of our homes. Even with optimal climate control, we still feel the instinctive need to be in secluded, cosy spaces in winter, and open, bright spaces in summer. Native Indians moved between summer and winter camps; why should we be so different in our sophisticated, modern environments? Where we once threw back our curtains to allow light to stream into a room or pulled them tightly closed to keep out the cold and the dark, we can now throw back our space divisions, or bring them back in, as required.

Both natural ventilation and al fresco living are also only a 'touch of a button' away, with inner courtyards and vast skylights that can be opened up to allow a sense of outdoor living whenever required – air quality permitting!

Technology introduces variety and adventure

Virtual reality is also playing a big part in our new homes. Any need for a change of scene can be indulged beyond simply altering the layout of our rooms and furniture. Configurations of screens carrying moving images can give us the impression of being in any number of different places – adrift under the stars at night, or looking out on the wonders of the Serengeti at dawn.

The art of sleeping

Sleeping will gradually cease to be confined to just one room, where a bed can be placed in only two or three possible positions. Beds are being designed in ever more creative forms that take the need for mobility into account. It is now feasible to vary sleeping areas seasonally, or even diurnally. The bed connoisseur can easily appoint the 'afternoon siesta spot', the 'nocturnal spot' and the 'Sunday-in-bed spot'.

Beds designed as intriguing units are at once aesthetically pleasing and practical. Moving an entire unit complete with light sources, technical gadgets and practical surfaces liberates us from the annoyance of having to move not only the bed, but also the night stands, bedside lights and clock radio.

Potential moving targets

Although mains services still determine the position of both kitchens and bathrooms within the layout of a home, technology will ultimately give us the means to vary the location of these spaces as well. Whether any of us will be inclined to implement this option remains to be seen: finding the bathroom in the middle of the night could involve some humorous consequences for more than just the youngest members of the household!

Bringing the outdoors in

The layout of our homes has, throughout history, been dictated by the most pressing needs of the time, whether it be warmth, security or aesthetics. Today, our home environment is under our personal control more than ever before: we shape and re-shape our surroundings to suit our moods and whims.

Our ancestors lived surrounded by nature and took it very much for granted. They focused their attention instead on conquests, inventions and the realization of dreams. Today we find that we need more than our man-made reality. Nature is a source of inspiration. Our new layouts reflect this: movement, curves and change are prized above the angular immobility of unchanging shapes and forms.

Natural light, fire and water have endured. We covet them in our homes above and beyond the passing thrill of the latest gadget. Where the latter can always be improved upon and replaced by the latest model, the ever-changing qualities of light, fire and water are timeless and fascinating to us. They will increasingly shape and define our homes because we need them to counteract the lifeless quality of the possessions that have come to dominate our lives.

Back to the drawing board

With a sense of the direction in which our homes are headed, let's now begin to explore in detail some of the many options available to you for reconfiguring your home.

HOW TO USE THIS BOOK

A guide to getting the most out of its plans and symbols

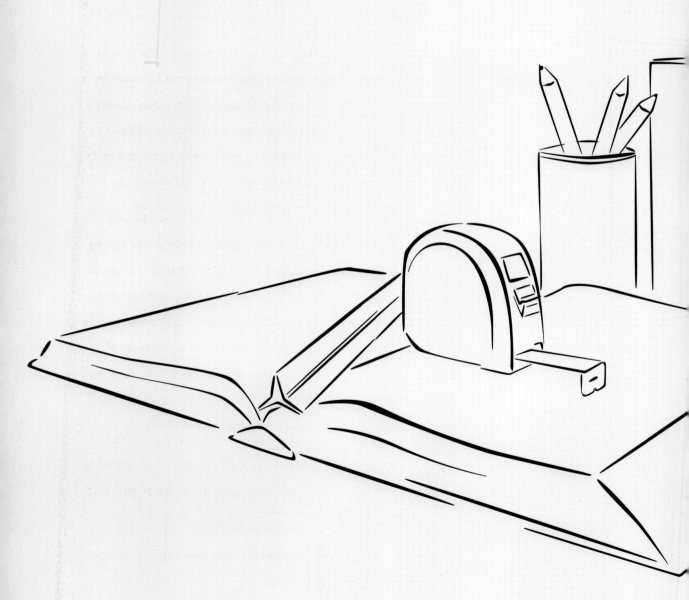

*L*ooking at a property on a plan is about as exciting as reading somebody else's shopping list – unless of course you happen to be an architect, designer, structural engineer or developer. To us, plans are fascinating and full of promise – a design to be analyzed, envisaged and usually pulled apart at the seams. But to onlookers, we're almost as sad as trainspotters!

Don't be put off if you draw a blank the first time you try to interpret a plan. The key point to realize is the fact that plans are limited to using only two dimensions to depict three-dimensional spaces. This is one of the most complex aspects of plan reading to master.

For example, trying to visualize a staircase – and how it relates to the floor immediately above or below it – can be a challenge, to say the least. Working out which way is up is hard enough, without having to envisage the appropriate three-dimensional image of the next floor that the staircase leads to. Understanding the less than obvious relationship between raised levels on the same floor can be equally difficult for the untrained eye.

It takes years of practice to be able to look at a plan and immediately get a three-dimensional mental image of what a property will look like and how large or small it will feel in reality.

In the meantime, here are a few tricks for grasping the gist of a plan and bringing it to life.

The three essential steps to understanding plans

STEP 1: FIND THE FRONT DOOR

The same principle applies to viewing a property on a plan as to walking through one in reality. When looking at a plan, start with the **front door** – not the window or the back staircase! You will then have a much better sense of the flow of the space and its general layout.

STEP 2: IDENTIFY THE EXTERNAL STRUCTURAL FEATURES

Once you have identified the front door, cast your eye over the plan and take note of all the main external structural features: **windows, walls, conservatory, garage, patio**. This will give you a good idea of the size and feel of the property as a whole.

STEP 3: IDENTIFY THE INTERNAL LAYOUT

Once you understand the property externally, allow your eye to wander – from the front door – through each of the rooms to give you a sense of the flow of the property and the amount of space available. Note features such as **internal doors, openings, built-in storage, mezzanines, staircases, pillars, structural beams** and **skylights**.Take it room by room, familiarizing yourself with the layout of the property. To make the reconfigured plans in this book quicker and easier to read, the areas are colour-coded. Then, having studied each room, you should see the property as a whole and how it fits together like a jigsaw puzzle.

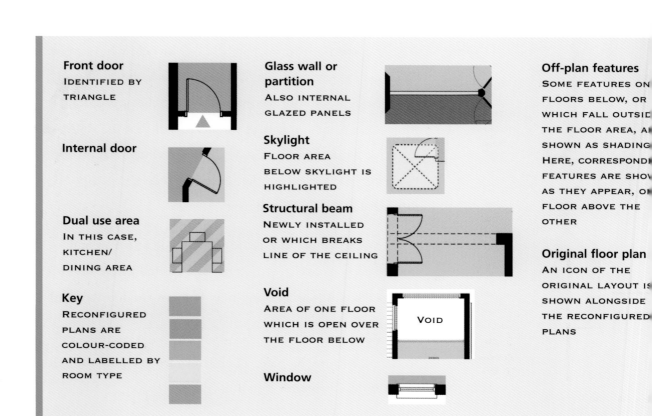

Front door
IDENTIFIED BY TRIANGLE

Internal door

Dual use area
IN THIS CASE, KITCHEN/DINING AREA

Key
RECONFIGURED PLANS ARE COLOUR-CODED AND LABELLED BY ROOM TYPE

Glass wall or partition
ALSO INTERNAL GLAZED PANELS

Skylight
FLOOR AREA BELOW SKYLIGHT IS HIGHLIGHTED

Structural beam
NEWLY INSTALLED OR WHICH BREAKS LINE OF THE CEILING

Void
AREA OF ONE FLOOR WHICH IS OPEN OVER THE FLOOR BELOW

VOID

Window

Off-plan features
SOME FEATURES ON FLOORS BELOW, OR WHICH FALL OUTSID THE FLOOR AREA, A SHOWN AS SHADING HERE, CORRESPONDI FEATURES ARE SHOV AS THEY APPEAR, O FLOOR ABOVE THE OTHER

Original floor plan
AN ICON OF THE ORIGINAL LAYOUT IS SHOWN ALONGSIDE THE RECONFIGURED PLANS

If you follow these three steps in order – 1) find the front door, 2) identify the external structural features, 3) identify the internal layout – you will find that properties will start to take shape before your eyes and make sense to you. Instead of being snow blind and confused, you will be able to visualize in easy stages.

Project by project

The projects in each chapter all follow the same format of original and revised plans and explanatory text.

The first two pages of each project show you the layout of the property before work started, together with bullet points describing:

▎ **existing problems,** highlighting the shortcomings or limitations of the space pre-transformation, and

▎ **objectives,** clarifying the client brief and the desirable end result.

The following pages of the project show you the reconfigured layout – or layouts if more than one solution was proposed – together with:

▎ **solutions,** with bullet points describing how the objectives were achieved, and

▎ an **icon** of the original plan alongside the final layout to help you compare one with the other without having to flick back to the start of each project.

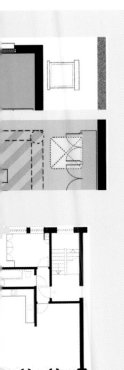

Scale

EACH SET OF RECONFIGURED PLANS HAS A KEY REPRESENTING THE SIZE IN METRES OF THE PLANS ON THAT PAGE. IF A PLAN DOES CONFORM TO A COMMONLY USED SCALE (1:25, 1:50, 1:100) IT IS ANNOTATED ACCORDINGLY

5M

Mezzanine or raised levels

FEATURES ON LEVELS BELOW ARE SHOWN IN SHADING

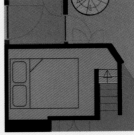

Staircases

ARROWS ALWAYS INDICATE DIRECTION UP A STAIRCASE. THESE DRAWINGS SHOW:

① STAIRS ARRIVING AT THIS LEVEL FROM BELOW

② STAIRS RUNNING FROM THIS POINT, RISING TO FLOOR ABOVE

③ CUT-AWAY THROUGH STAIRS RISING TO FLOOR ABOVE

④ STAIRS RISING FROM FLOOR BELOW, REVEALED BY CUT-AWAY OF FLIGHT RISING TO FLOOR ABOVE

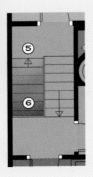

⑤ SHORT ARROWS INDICATE STAIRS ARRIVING AT HALF-LANDING OR RAISED LEVEL

⑥ SHADED AREA INDICATES OPEN AREA OVER STAIRS BELOW

VALUABLE SPACE

Redefining existing space to increase property value

*O*ne thing that we have all learned from watching property developers at work is that nothing makes a property's value skyrocket quite like the creation of additional rooms. In many countries, developers and homeowners alike have all too often taken the principle to extremes: the resulting properties frequently look more like rabbit warrens, with small rooms linked by tortuous corridors, than the well-designed homes that they should be. The secret is to know the limitations of your property. Carving up the floor space to achieve maximum value needs to be balanced against quality of living and aesthetics. An even balance between these three will still secure long-term gain, but without neglecting the here-and-now.

Imagination and lateral thinking are the key tools that you need to successfully transform a property into valuable space. The most difficult task you face as a current homeowner looking to remodel your property is seeing the space objectively. You will have become accustomed to it and you will tend to take the good with the bad, with equal resignation. The trick is to see the property with fresh eyes and to look at it as an outsider would: with dispassion and objectivity.

Even if you are purchasing a new home and plan to transform it, the task is far from easy. There are so many other considerations to take into account beyond the actual layout and how you might transform it that it is easy to get sidetracked.

Before going too deeply into our current dilemmas, let's take a quick look at some of the issues that we will be facing in the near future, and how we will be creating our valuable space then. The basic principle of what follows may be of great use as you consider your property now, especially if either the view from or the location of your property are less than ideal and causing you concern.

Looking ahead

A glance at the long term points to the fact that our current issues in creating valuable space may seem minor as the century progresses and new challenges present themselves.

The importance of internal layout and learning to make the very most of the space available will be vital as our homes evolve. Getting the framework right now will help us to adapt our homes more easily in the future.

Our ideals versus long-term reality Our biggest problem will probably be that our ideals and the reality will continue to drift further apart. A growing population and a shortage of property will force us to redevelop areas that fall far short of our ideals. Inevitably, the reality of the brownfield site is looming.

An interesting nationwide survey in Britain recently tried to establish whether the views and schemes of architects and planners were in keeping with what the public really wanted in a new home. To the dismay of the architects, it found that what people coveted more than anything was the 'executive home' with a 'big roof, big garden and big double garage'. Most people felt that traffic pollution and over-congested roads were vital issues to be dealt with, but they still wanted the use of at least one car at all times. They agreed that destroying the countryside in order to satisfy the urban spread was deplorable, but they still aspired to live in a large detached house with plenty of garden.

THE MINIATURE ROCK GARDEN PRINCIPLE

Indoor miniature rock gardens may not be to everybody's taste, but don't dismiss the concept out of hand. If living in a city means that you can't have a garden or any outdoor space, why not have a mini-garden in your flat – tiny, easily maintained and more diverse than a house plant or two?

Ultimately, we'll all have to make compromises when the population threatens to outgrow the available living space. While it's unlikely that we will all rush out and purchase miniature rock gardens at that point, we will nonetheless have to transform our homes to accommodate the pace of change. It's a matter of adapting to reality and making the very best of what we have, within constraints that everybody would rather be without.

THE DREADED BROWNFIELD SITE

Eventually, we will have to redevelop brownfield sites, especially in the cities and surrounding suburbs, regardless of the short-term financial implications. Lateral thinking will be essential in developing habitable internal spaces on these sites. Their surroundings are often ugly and unappealing, so it will become increasingly necessary to turn the occupants' view inwards as opposed to outwards. The value of the property will rely heavily on its internal configuration and finish.

LOOKING IN, NOT OUT

Entire buildings will be designed and built without a single window looking out onto the outside world. Instead, each room will give onto an inner courtyard flooded with natural daylight. These new-style courtyards will either be open to the sky or glazed over and insulated at the touch of a button. The variety will be limited only by the footprint of the site and the imagination of the occupants: an inner garden, a decorative or recreational pool, a sculpture set against a stark backdrop, a sports area, a maze, an amphitheatre.

The added bonus of buildings that turn in on themselves is the privacy – the outside world is forgotten as soon as the threshold to the inner sanctuary is crossed.

Adjusting to the shock

Large windows that let in lots of light and have expansive views are part of our ideal – and one of the major selling points of many properties. There is a natural concern that turning the focus inwards will engender a feeling of being trapped. Our challenge is to make the internal view both uplifting and inspiring. Finding ingenious ways to filter as much daylight as possible into closed internal spaces is essential. Skylights and glazed panels in unexpected places can go a long way towards alleviating the feeling of claustrophobia.

Back to the drawing board

We don't have to start looking inwards just yet. However, unless you live in a conservation area in a city or own land in the country, you will always be faced with the possibility that your current view may be marred by the construction of another building.

A room with an internal view

How many of us have prided ourselves on our fine view only to find that planning permission has been granted for some monstrosity to be built right under our noses? The thought of looking straight into your neighbours' windows can be less than inspiring!

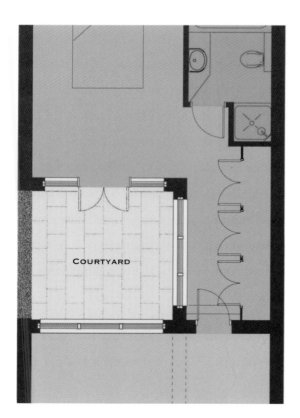

COURTYARD

The key in this case is to make sure that the focus is turned inwards. An internal courtyard filled with plants – and daylight from above – is ideal, as it brings in a sense of the outdoors.

If possible, creating a central focal point to the home itself – or, alternatively, to each room – distracts the eye and gets over the problem. The possibilities are numerous. Think fire, water, nature: a central fireplace, a water feature, an inner garden or large tree. Even a striking piece of sculpture will do – anything that is large enough to draw the eye and that works within the space.

Valuable space is not just room creation

The 'behind-the-scenes' details count for more than most people realize when it comes to selling a property – not to mention actually living in it. These details may not be immediately obvious; instead, they become apparent as you spend more time in the property.

Creating new rooms literally transforms the space in a home, but it's only one (albeit the most obvious) of the many elements that go into adding true value to a property.

Climate control

One element that is often overlooked in European homes is climate control. Creating a spatially well-proportioned home with all the comforts but neglecting climate control is like dressing and forgetting to put your shoes on.

Our changing climate and unpredictable weather patterns mean that we need to address our air conditioning/heating capacity now, not leave it for some future unspecified time. Modern technology has given us air conditioning and heating that can be centralized, with discreet vents in either the floors or walls of each room to pump out cold or hot air as the season requires. Installing these central air systems can be costly in older homes, although it is standard in all high-specification new-build properties in America, for instance.

When it comes to your own home, choosing to install an air-conditioning system is a decision based on budget and long-term comfort. If you plan to stay for several years, it may be well worth the investment: hot summers will suddenly become very bearable, and air conditioning is an excellent selling point if and when you eventually sell. Losing unsightly radiators will also help the look of the property and make furniture arrangement easier.

BUDGET VERSUS VALUE

If you are wondering whether it is worth using limited funds to install air conditioning, consider how hot your home is likely to get in the summer months.

Any property that faces south, west or south-west will be an oven in a heatwave, as it will have the full force of the sun from midday onwards. Cross-ventilation created by windows opposite each other (within a room or between two rooms) will help to cool things down, unless there is no natural breeze.

The higher the property, the hotter it will get: a top-floor flat in a conversion will be much hotter than a basement flat in the same house. Decide how unbearable it is likely to be in the heat and make your decisions about air conditioning accordingly.

On the other hand, don't go and choose a north-facing basement flat for its 'cool factor' in summer – remember long, dreary, cold winters and think twice before you make that summer purchase.

KEEPING IT WARM UNDERFOOT

With the growing popularity of uncarpeted space, providing adequate warmth in winter is an important consideration. Stone, tile and any number of other hard surfaces may be refreshingly cool to walk on in summer, but can be very chilly in the depths of winter. Underfloor heating is certainly tricky and costly to install, but it will go a long way towards giving a high-spec feel to your home – not to mention increasing the resale value.

Valuable means peace and quiet

Imagine a beautifully laid-out home, perfectly finished and giving the impression of high-value space. This image would be totally destroyed if you could hear not only what was going on in other rooms within the property, but also the sound of your neighbours. Value immediately goes out of the window when soundproofing has not been appropriately addressed. Plasterboard partition walls are not soundproof. Solid structural walls are soundproof, as it is harder for sound to travel through them. Any floor surface – unless it is carpeted – will carry sound rather than block it. Adding soundproofing to partition walls is possible, but is usually only feasible before the walls are plastered and decorated.

SOFT FURNISHINGS CAN HELP

Bear in mind that the more fabric you have in a room, the more sound is absorbed. A room with a wooden floor, Venetian blinds at the windows and minimal furniture will echo and carry the slightest sound. By contrast, a room with carpet (even rugs), full-length lined and interlined curtains, sofas and a lot of soft furnishings will muffle all sound.

THE 'PADDED CELL' SOLUTION

Further up the scale of costs of soundproofing would be to 'fabric' the walls of one or several rooms. Wool is highly recommended for soundproofing, although more costly than, say, heavy-duty cottons. Behind the face fabric, the normal installation procedure includes battening and padding the walls. Instead of just using padding, you could also add soundproofing material behind the main fabric.

This is particularly effective when you also 'fabric' the ceiling. Acoustic tiles can be fixed to the ceiling underneath the fabric, thereby minimizing sound from the floor immediately above.

WHITE NOISE

Turning for a moment to technology, consider the white noise option. White noise is a noise that contains all frequencies and so effectively masks out other sounds. This is a solution often used in office environments where noise pollution can be a serious problem and can adversely affect staff performance.

White noise is not a cheap solution for the home, and is something that requires calling in the experts. But it will be money well spent, especially if it proves to be the only effective soundproofing tool for the property.

Light levels Not all properties benefit from good light, and therefore 'cheating' is essential to create effective, high-value space. Dark properties are always difficult to sell and they are never easy to live in either. Sunlight – and light in general – is essential to our well-being. Only nocturnal creatures thrive in the dark.

Balance is vital here: creating a well-lit space is not about installing a lot of light fittings. Football stadiums are not the look of the future! Instead, creative and subtle lighting is

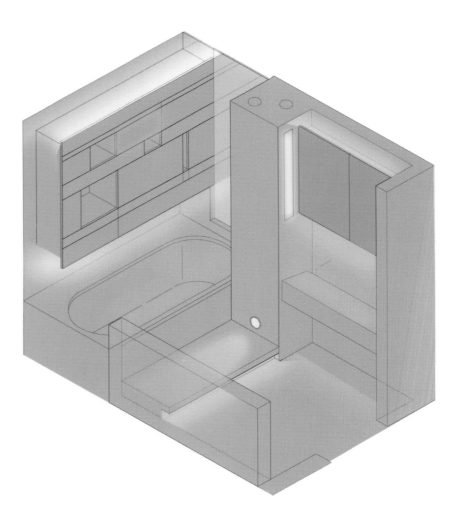

the way forward. Concealed lighting, as opposed to direct lighting, creates mood and atmosphere while still getting the light levels of a room up. It also helps to create a sense of depth to a space: when you are unsure where one surface stops and another begins, a space becomes at once interesting and intriguing.

Adding lighting in unexpected places is ideal for windowless bathrooms. Concealed lighting above and below cabinets, storage units and raised platforms washes the walls and floor with light. An opaque panel can also bring in light from another room to help to open up the space. Contrast all these subtle lighting devices with a pin prick or two of light from skirting lighting as a final touch to the overall moody effect.

BACK-LIT DOORS

Concealed lighting is extremely versatile. Consider deploying it behind sandblasted glass cupboard doors – this will give added depth to the room as well as additional light, and it draws the eye immediately. Using different colours for the lighting can have a novel effect, although white light does take a lot of beating.

All the details add up Keep a close eye on all of the 'behind-the-scenes' details as well as room creation and you are sure to be creating high-value space. These details will improve the living quality of your home and will pay dividends when you come to sell the property.

Creating a luxury duplex out of two apartments

CONCEPT: PAULA ROBINSON DESIGN GROUP

When the owner of this top-floor, two-bedroom, two-bathroom apartment was offered the opportunity to purchase the one-bedroom, one-bathroom apartment immediately below him, he saw the chance to create one very versatile – and valuable – duplex.

His top-floor apartment consisted of an open-plan reception room, a kitchen, two small bedrooms, an en-suite bathroom, a shower room and a huge roof terrace that spanned the length of the property. The one-bedroom apartment that he was about to purchase offered a large living room, a dining room, a kitchen, a utility room, a bathroom and a bedroom.

In amalgamating the two apartments, the client wanted to create a duplex that would be as open-plan and versatile as possible. He required a combination of maximum entertaining space, accommodation for guests and, most importantly, increased property value.

Existing problems

- the **entrance lobby** of the top-floor two-bedroom apartment did not comply with Fire Regulations

- the apartment's **kitchen** had recently been installed and, although small for a future duplex, was to remain untouched

- the **two bedrooms** of the top-floor apartment were small and cramped

- the access to the **roof terrace** was via a steep, narrow staircase, which meant that the outdoor space was rarely used

- the one-bedroom apartment had good-sized, but old-fashioned, reception rooms

- the **kitchen** was badly configured

- the **bedroom** and the **bathroom** of the one-bedroom apartment were small

ORIGINAL LOWER FLOOR PLAN

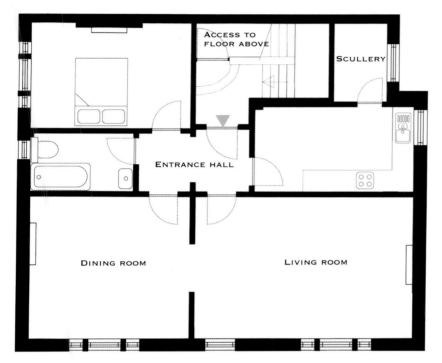

ACCESS TO FLOOR ABOVE

SCULLERY

ENTRANCE HALL

DINING ROOM

LIVING ROOM

ORIGINAL UPPER FLOOR PLAN

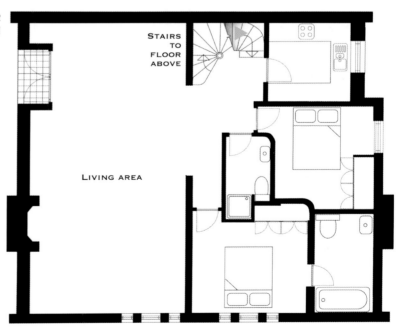

STAIRS TO FLOOR ABOVE

LIVING AREA

Objectives

▮ to transform two separate apartments
  into one duplex

▮ to make maximum use of the space
  available to create a contemporary,
  open-plan living space

▮ to make use of the large roof terrace

▮ to create luxurious space with
  increased value

A master suite with two fireplaces

The design concept for the lower floor of the new duplex apartment focused on a huge master suite, complete with its own sleeping, bathing and living areas. The areas are divided by floor-to-ceiling units in the centre of the suite: the living area is divided from the bathing area by a unit housing a separate toilet and separate shower; the bathing area is divided from the sleeping area by a second unit housing storage and closets. The master suite was designed around the apartment's two impressive existing fireplaces at opposite ends of the building, and two sets of French doors that led out onto two small balconies. The suite has two separate entrance doors and at the heart of the room is a bath/hot tub set in a limestone floor.

At first glance, the remainder of this floor consists of a large, curved hallway with a sweeping staircase leading up to the top floor of the duplex. A separate double bedroom and a bathroom with bath and separate shower complete the first floor. The only clue that this floor can be transformed into a three-bedroom, two-bathroom space is the fact that the second bathroom has two entrances – one leading into the hallway and one giving onto the living area of the master suite.

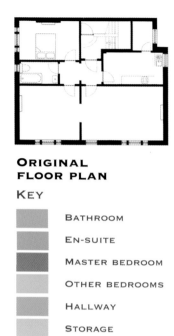

ORIGINAL FLOOR PLAN

KEY

- BATHROOM
- EN-SUITE
- MASTER BEDROOM
- OTHER BEDROOMS
- HALLWAY
- STORAGE

SEE ALSO PAGE 213 FOR THE ORIGINAL CONCEPT OF THIS BATHROOM LAYOUT

- the **front door** to the apartment has been relocated to borrow additional space from the communal stairs

- the small entrance hall has been transformed into a grand **entrance**, complete with curved wall and large sweeping staircase leading to the top floor of the duplex

- the living room has now become the **living area of the master suite**, complete with large fireplace

- a floor-to-ceiling central unit divides the living area from the master suite's **bathing area**. This unit houses a **separate toilet** on one side and a **separate shower** on the other side. In the centre of the bathing area is a free-standing bath/hot tub.

OPTION 1
MASTER SUITE MODE

- the second central unit houses the double basin vanity unit and storage. This unit divides the bathing area from the **sleeping area** of the master suite, with a fireplace and built-in closets. This area was formerly the dining room and bathroom

- a structural support beam replaces the wall that once divided the dining room from the living room

- the **second bedroom** remains where the original bedroom was in the one-bedroom apartment

- the **second bathroom** takes up an area formerly occupied by the utility room and part of the former kitchen. It has two entrance doors, one from the hallway and one from the living area of the master suite

0   5M

A master suite transforms into an extra bedroom

The client's brief to have a luxurious, self-contained master suite, three additional bedrooms and two additional bathrooms in an open-plan, spacious duplex presented some dilemmas. The number of bedrooms was an important issue, not just to house the frequent and numerous guests, but also for resale purposes. The client was not willing to compromise on either spacious feel or value.

The master suite was therefore created to be as luxurious and spacious as possible, but with the ability to be divided, as required, into a further bedroom. The first central unit, which divides the master suite's living area from its bathing area, also houses two etched glass walls that can slide out and be locked into place. This then turns the living area into a third bedroom for this floor of the duplex. The bedroom has access to its own en-suite bathroom, although the latter can also be used by bedroom 2, sited across the entrance hall. Bedroom 3 has its own entrance from the entrance hall – formerly the entrance to the living area of the master suite.

While the client preferred the option of a sofa bed for the living area/bedroom 3, it would be entirely possible to have a built-in wall bed in the dividing central unit. This could be pulled down as required. An easily moved sofa would then also form part of the furnishings. This could be positioned in front of the windows when the bed was down and moved back opposite the fireplace when the bed was concealed.

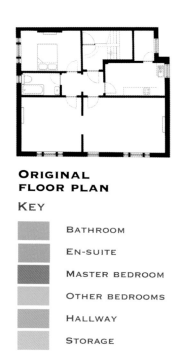

ORIGINAL FLOOR PLAN

KEY

▨	BATHROOM
▨	EN-SUITE
▨	MASTER BEDROOM
▨	OTHER BEDROOMS
▨	HALLWAY
▨	STORAGE

SEE ALSO PAGE 213 FOR THE ORIGINAL CONCEPT OF THIS BATHROOM LAYOUT

OPTION 2
3 BEDROOM MODE

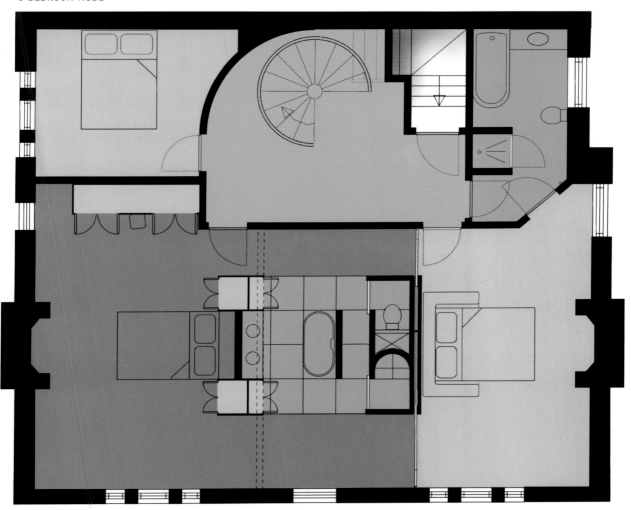

- the living area of the master suite now transforms itself into **bedroom 3**. Two sliding acoustic panels pull out from the unit that divides the space from the master suite's bathing area to lock into place and form the walls between bedroom 3 and the master en-suite. A sofa bed opens out to provide guest accommodation in bedroom 3.

- the second bathroom now becomes the en-suite bathroom for bedroom 3. A second door into the entrance hall means that this bathroom is also still accessible to bedroom 2

- the master suite's **bathing area** remains unchanged in this configuration except for the addition of two walls on either side of the toilet and shower that divide the area from the newly formed bedroom 3

- the **sleeping area** remains unchanged.

- bedroom 2's position remains unchanged

0   5M

An open, airy entertaining floor

The top floor of the duplex is a huge, open-plan space with a kitchen, a third bathroom and an area that can be closed off to become a small study or a fourth bedroom. Two fireplaces dominate the main entertaining space along with an additional feature: a large, automated skylight has been carved out of the floor of the long terrace. This not only brings additional light to the space, but can also be fully opened to give the dining area of the top floor of the duplex an al fresco feel.

ORIGINAL FLOOR PLAN

REVISED UPPER FLOOR

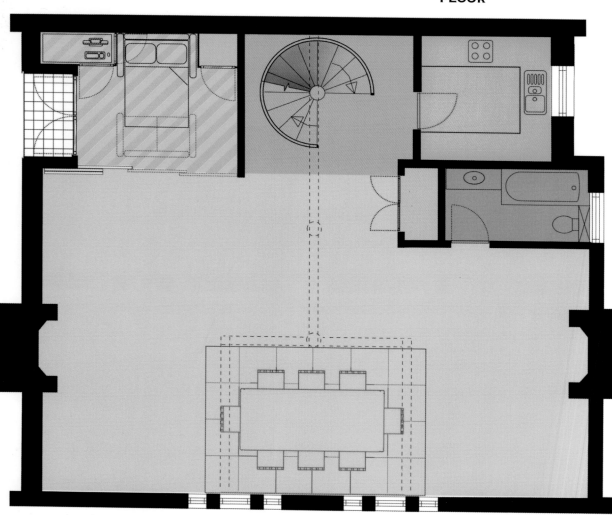

- the **kitchen** remains in its original configuration, as it had been newly re-fitted and was not to be touched for budget reasons

- **bathroom 3** provides facilities for the living area and bedroom 4 when required

- the **study/bedroom 4** takes up a quiet corner of the large top floor of the duplex and has access to its own small balcony. Acoustic panels slide across from a discreet position against the wall to form either a study or a bedroom as required. The built-in **workstation** slides into the left side unit when in use as a bedroom. The sofa bed is then placed in the empty alcove. The workstation remains accessible via the closet door

- the large **open-plan living area** has two big fireplaces at either end of the room. The roof terrace has had an automated skylight installed, bringing light to the whole open-plan entertainment area of the duplex. On fine days it offers al fresco dining for the limestone paved dining area

- additional closets have been provided at the top of the stairs

REVISED TERRACE

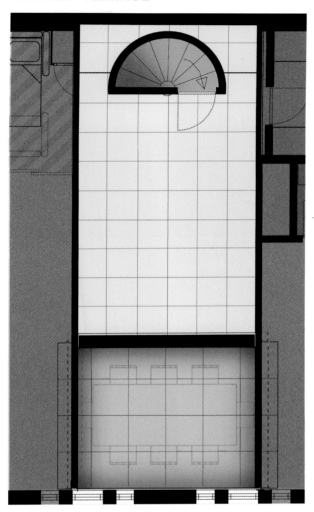

KEY

BATHROOM

BEDROOM

HALLWAY

KITCHEN

LIVING AREA

STORAGE

STUDY AREA

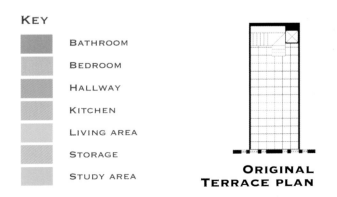

ORIGINAL TERRACE PLAN

0   5M

Muse as WWII mews meets 21st century

ARCHITECT: SPENCE HARRIS HOGAN

This two storey end-of-terrace mews house was originally built as stables in Victorian times, but had to be rebuilt after bomb damage in World War II. It had remained untouched since that time, but its prime location in a conservation area made it an ideal candidate for reconfiguration. On the ground floor it had a living room, dining room, kitchen, toilet, storage area, garage and tiny courtyard. The first floor had three small bedrooms, a bathroom and a separate toilet. The entire configuration of the property felt small, boxy and dark.

Existing problems

- the **front door** was set back from the front of the house, reducing any natural daylight

- the **corridor** was long, narrow and gloomy

- the **dining room** had poor natural light, making it a dim and dingy room

- the **kitchen** only had a skylight to provide daylight

- the **courtyard** was wasted space as, despite benefiting from light from its glazed roof, it was too small to be an effective indoor area

- the **master bedroom** had no en-suite facility

- the other two **bedrooms** were small

- the only **bathroom** had a separate toilet, making it very dated

- the property's **flat roof** was wasted space

Objectives

- to make maximum use of the space available, including the courtyard area and flat roof

- to maximize light and a sense of space within the property

- to redesign the front entrance to maximize space and light

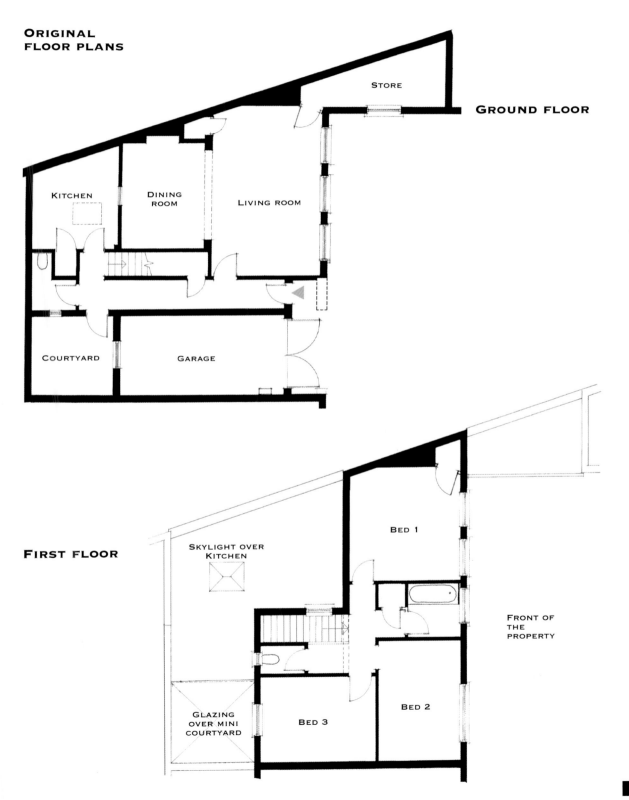

**ORIGINAL
FLOOR PLANS**

STORE

GROUND FLOOR

KITCHEN

DINING
ROOM

LIVING ROOM

COURTYARD

GARAGE

FIRST FLOOR

SKYLIGHT OVER
KITCHEN

BED 1

FRONT OF
THE
PROPERTY

GLAZING
OVER MINI
COURTYARD

BED 3

BED 2

Swapping the upstairs and downstairs was the key to a successful result

The façade was reconfigured to bring the garage and front doors flush with the front of the building, which gained floor space and additional light. Internally, the property was turned on its head to create a practical, light-filled, contemporary space. The three bedrooms moved down to the ground floor with a fine sweep of:

ORIGINAL GROUND FLOOR PLAN

- the **master bedroom** located in the reclaimed courtyard area and part of the former long garage. The new generous space is lit from above by an electric skylight that can be fully opened. A long line of built-in closets completes the suite

- the **en-suite bathroom** takes the place of the former gloomy kitchen. The bathroom is fully equipped with double basin vanity unit, toilet and bidet, bath and separate circular shower with skylight above. A window was also added in the

boundary wall, planning permission having been gained, making the en-suite a light-filled space

- **bedroom 2** takes up part of the former living room, enjoying daylight from two front-facing windows

- **bathroom 2** has been cleverly carved out of the former store room and is fully equipped with bath, basin and toilet, and has a window

- **bedroom 3** occupies what was once the gloomy dining room. Planning permission was gained to add a window in the boundary wall, making the room habitable. To overcome the bathroom dilemma, a shower and basin are included in bedroom 3 with:

  – a **separate toilet,** which serves bedroom 3 as well as general use. It also benefits from a window

SIDE ELEVATION OF STAIRCASE

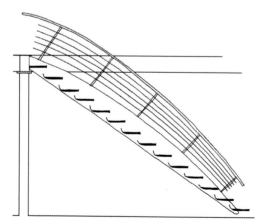

REVISED GROUND FLOOR LAYOUT

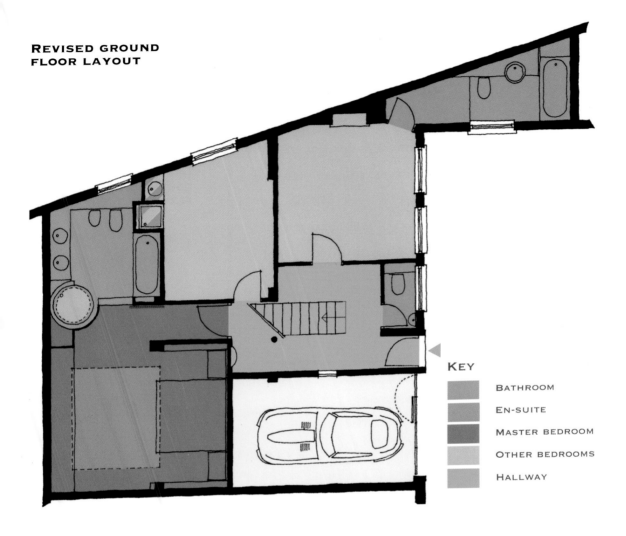

KEY

- BATHROOM
- EN-SUITE
- MASTER BEDROOM
- OTHER BEDROOMS
- HALLWAY

REVISED FRONT AND GARAGE DOOR POSITIONS

BRINGING THE GARAGE AND FRONT DOORS FLUSH WITH THE FRONT OF THE BUILDING ADDED FLOOR SPACE AND BRIGHTENED THE PREVIOUSLY GLOOMY HALLWAY

OLD

NEW

0   5M

Making the best of unused flat roof space

The open, floating staircase is the perfect introduction to the fresh, open-plan living space on the first floor. The former boxy bedrooms have given way to a light-filled space complete with sun deck and skylights. Increased floor space on this first floor was reclaimed from the formerly wasted flat roof area immediately above the old dining room and kitchen. This reconfiguration of space has resulted in a first floor plan that is no longer misshapen and constricted, and certainly contributes to the overall value of the property. The first floor now presents itself with:

ORIGINAL FIRST FLOOR PLAN

KEY

- HALLWAY
- LIVING AREA
- KITCHEN
- WINDOWS/ GLASS

- the **staircase,** which was specially designed to draw visitors immediately up to the first floor living space from the entrance below. It is a semi-cantilevered stair, reminiscent of an ocean liner gangway and inspired by Frank Lloyd Wright's 'bouncing' stairs

- the **kitchen** welcomes you to the new entertainment floor, and is now spacious and well designed

- the **dining area** benefits from both a new skylight above and newly installed French doors opening onto an ornamental balcony at the front of the building. This adds interest and character to both the interior and the façade itself

- the **living area** flows between the dining area and the sun deck, benefiting from maximum light and space. Steps and double doors lead out onto:
  - the **sun deck,** which is a generous outdoor space. It includes a cheeky round skylight that directly overlooks the circular shower in the master bathroom on the floor below. Beyond the sun deck, the large, electric skylight overlooks the master bedroom

**REVISED FIRST
FLOOR LAYOUT**

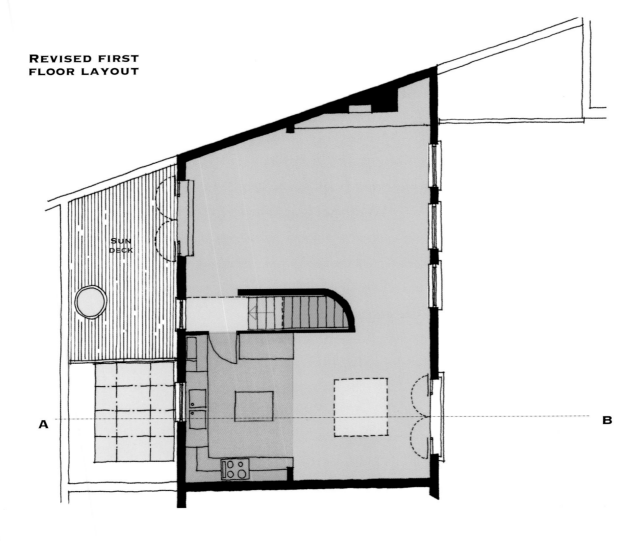

SUN
DECK

A ⸱ ⸱ ⸱ ⸱ ⸱ ⸱ ⸱ ⸱ ⸱ ⸱ ⸱ ⸱ ⸱ ⸱ ⸱ ⸱ ⸱ ⸱ B

**SECTION
THROUGH
BUILDING**

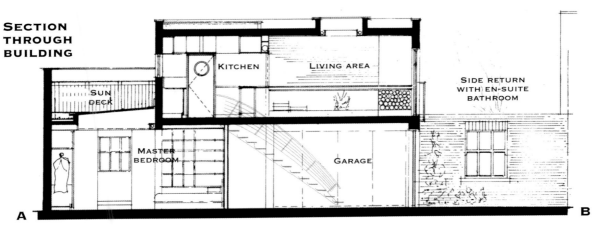

SUN
DECK

KITCHEN   LIVING AREA

SIDE RETURN
WITH EN-SUITE
BATHROOM

MASTER
BEDROOM

GARAGE

A   B

0   5M

Moving into the basement – thanks to an unusual layout

DESIGNERS: PAULA ROBINSON DESIGN GROUP

This three level terraced house was unusual in two ways. Firstly, it included a 'direct' access way to the rear of the property. These access routes normally take the form of simple periodic gaps between rows of terraced houses. However, this property's rear reception room, used as the dining room, extended over the access way to butt up to the next property. The resulting access 'tunnel' led under this room, through a cellar, to the rear. The second unusual feature was that the cellar extended the full width of the property, rather than being confined to the area below the entrance hall.

The property had previously been split into two apartments: the slightly raised ground floor with cellar and garden, and the top two floors. The larger than usual rear reception room of this lower apartment was used as a living room, with bedroom to the front and minuscule bathroom at the rear, accessed through the kitchen.

Existing problems

- the property needed to be reconfigured to achieve a more **practical layout**

- the **living room** had originally been the dining room of the property when it was a complete house. As a living room in the converted one-bedroom apartment, it lost the advantage of the impressive square bay window at the front of the property

- while the **bedroom** benefited from period features, it felt less than private, being divided from the living room only by folding doors

- the **kitchen** was a good size, but walking through it to reach the bathroom was less than ideal

- space was lost from the **bathroom** to the mandatory lobby dividing kitchen and bathroom

- the **cellar**, whilst being a large appealing space, had only 1.8m head height, interrupted by pipes and services

ORIGINAL FLOOR PLAN

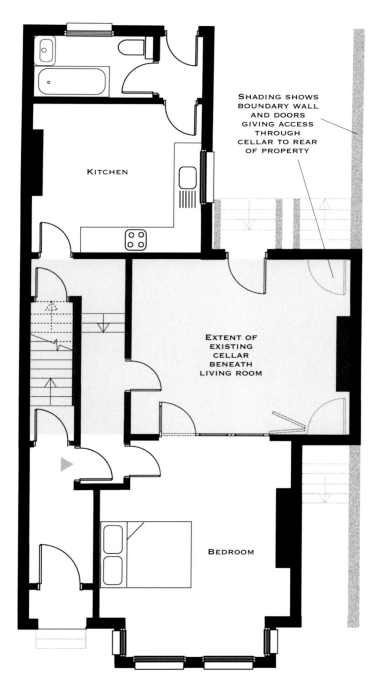

SHADING SHOWS BOUNDARY WALL AND DOORS GIVING ACCESS THROUGH CELLAR TO REAR OF PROPERTY

KITCHEN

EXTENT OF EXISTING CELLAR BENEATH LIVING ROOM

BEDROOM

Objectives

▮ to reconfigure the property to create a contemporary living space with increased value

▮ to increase the size of the bathroom and make it more accessible from the bedroom

▮ to make use of the larger than usual cellar and incorporate it into the apartment's living space

A clever staircase and dealing with the foundations

The key to redesigning this one-bedroom apartment into a contemporary living space with increased value was turning the cellar into habitable space. The design involved the excavation of the cellar to give full head height and then transforming it into a large kitchen/breakfast room. Strengthening the foundations at the deepest excavations meant the staircase had to turn away from the wall as it met the lower level. Use of fully glazed doors, one opening to the garden and one to a skylit corridor to the front, let in natural light.

This allowed the ground floor to be reconfigured into comfortable, free-flowing space. The front of the property returned to its original intended use with two reception rooms. The folding doors between the two reception rooms allows them to be used as either one large open-plan room or as two separate rooms. The old kitchen has been replaced by a bedroom with built-in closets and an en-suite bathroom, with a door leading into the garden.

ORIGINAL FLOOR PLAN

KEY

	EN-SUITE
	BEDROOM
	KITCHEN
	HALLWAY
	LIVING AREA
	STORAGE

- the bedroom has returned to its original intended use as the **living room,** with double doors leading to:
  - the **dining room/second reception room,** which had previously been the living room. The doors can be folded back to create one large reception room
- the former kitchen has become the **bedroom,** with built-in closets and:

- the **en-suite bathroom** with recessed double-ended bath and shower and single basin vanity unit. The boxed-in toilet cistern has been positioned to conceal the toilet and create a mock corridor to the garden door

- the **cellar** has been excavated to give full head height and has been transformed into the kitchen/breakfast room, with access into the garden and to the front of the property

REVISED FLOOR LAYOUTS

BASEMENT

GROUND FLOOR

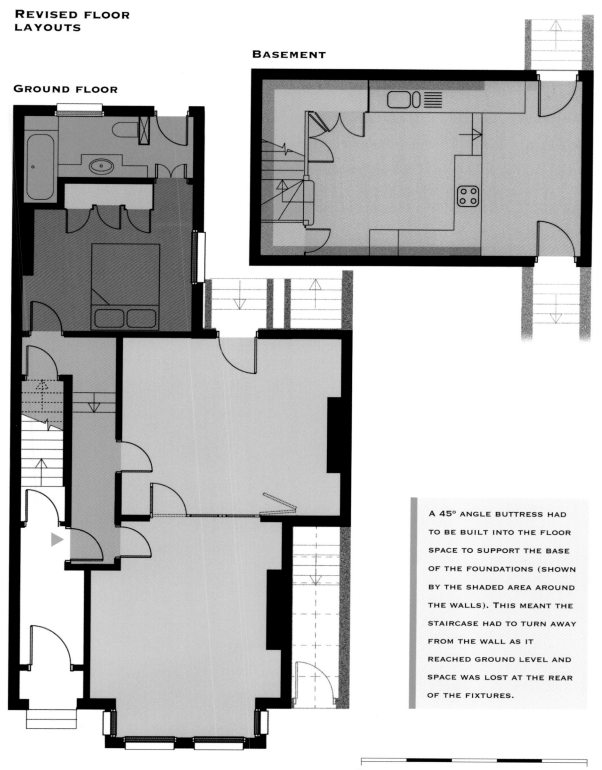

A 45° ANGLE BUTTRESS HAD TO BE BUILT INTO THE FLOOR SPACE TO SUPPORT THE BASE OF THE FOUNDATIONS (SHOWN BY THE SHADED AREA AROUND THE WALLS). THIS MEANT THE STAIRCASE HAD TO TURN AWAY FROM THE WALL AS IT REACHED GROUND LEVEL AND SPACE WAS LOST AT THE REAR OF THE FIXTURES.

0   5M

Tiny pre-war terrace expanded to offer 21st century space

ARCHITECT: HUGH BROUGHTON

This property was almost a classic example of the British 'two up, two down', which refers to a house with two rooms on the ground floor and two rooms on the first floor.

This tiny house was built at the start of the 20th century, with an entrance hall, a small living room and a kitchen/breakfast room with a separate scullery on the ground floor. It actually had three bedrooms plus a bathroom on the first floor, instead of the classic two bedrooms. However, the third bedroom was so small that it could barely accommodate more than a single bed and a bedside cabinet.

Existing problems

- the **entrance hall** was long, dark, narrow and wasteful of space

- the **kitchen/breakfast room** needed to be rethought for contemporary living

- the small outdated **scullery** made an unsightly access route to the garden

- the **master bedroom** was not served by an en-suite bathroom

- one **bathroom** served all three bedrooms

- **bedroom 3** was too small

- the property generally was too small to accommodate the family

- it was in desperate need of major remodelling and upgrading

ORIGINAL FLOOR PLANS

GROUND FLOOR

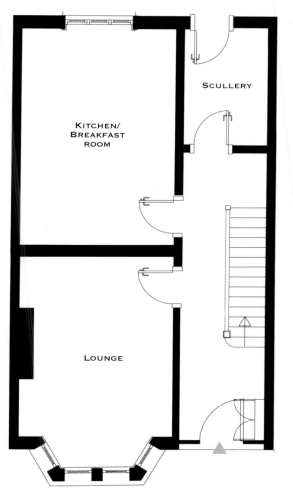

SCULLERY

KITCHEN/
BREAKFAST
ROOM

LOUNGE

FIRST FLOOR

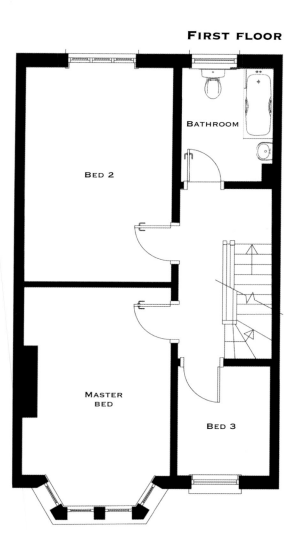

BATHROOM

BED 2

MASTER
BED

BED 3

Objectives

▮ to reconfigure the property to meet the
contemporary needs of a family with three children

▮ to upgrade the property as a whole

▮ to extend the space wherever possible

▮ to add an additional bedroom and shower room,
together with additional storage

▮ to remove the plastic lean-to conservatory

Stretching the property in depth and height

The solution for this property was to stretch its boundaries to the maximum. On ground-floor level, the old-fashioned 'two down' has given way to a new contemporary 'two down' space for modern, open-plan family living. The old plastic lean-to conservatory was demolished, and a substantial steel framework was buried into the walls, floor and ceiling to enable the creation of a new seven metre by five metre room to the rear of the house.

The old kitchen/breakfast room and scullery vanished, to be replaced by one large room. Clear, double-glazed folding doors lead out into the outdoor space – making the room feel even larger during the summer months with the doors thrown back completely. Skylights above bring more light into the interior of the room, ensuring that it has no dark or gloomy corners.

Part of the overly long original corridor now has a new role as a downstairs toilet and utility room, accessed from the kitchen area. This makes the new entrance corridor shorter and, consequently, it feels more inviting.

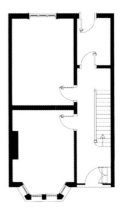

ORIGINAL GROUND FLOOR PLAN

KEY

■	BATHROOM
■	KITCHEN
■	HALLWAY
■	LIVING AREA
■	STORAGE
■	UTILITY ROOM

REVISED GROUND FLOOR LAYOUT

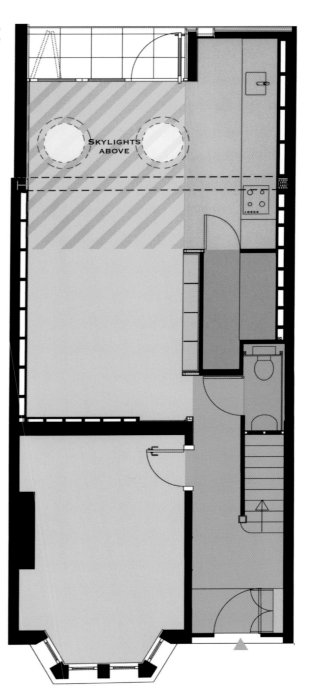

SKYLIGHTS ABOVE

■ the **entrance corridor** is now shorter than before with the addition of the new utility room and toilet to utilize what was formerly wasted space

■ the **living room** has been refurbished and retained as a more traditional-style intimate space in contrast to the new family room and kitchen area

■ the **family room/kitchen area** is awash with light from clear, double-glazed folding doors into the outdoor space, skylights and additional windows

■ the **utility room** is made all but invisible by a full-height bookcase built into a wall

■ the **outdoor space** is more obvious seen through full-height glazed doors and feels part of the living space during the summer months when the doors are folded back completely

0   5M

A new life aloft

The logic for the space on the upper floor was that the three children could easily share one bathroom and there was no need for any en-suite facility. Built-in cupboards were added to the former master bedroom and bedroom two, together with an invaluable cupboard accessed from the landing.

The master suite needed to be located above, with an en-suite facility. A roof extension was built to the full width of the house to provide a master bedroom with built-in double closets, an en-suite shower room and loft storage. This extension was designed with windows spanning side to side to maximize light penetration, and a skylight over the staircase to allow daylight to the first floor landing.

REVISED FIRST FLOOR LAYOUT

**ORIGINAL FIRST
FLOOR PLAN**

- the **first floor landing** benefits from daylight thanks to a skylight in the roof extension. It also has a new storage cupboard

- the master bedroom has been relocated to the new **roof extension,** turning the former master bedroom into:
  - **bedroom 2** with built-in closets

- **bedroom 3** formerly bedroom 2 also has built-in closets

- **bedroom 4** formerly bedroom 3 remains unchanged and is ideal for the youngest member of the household

- the **bathroom** has been refurbished but its position remains as before

- the **master suite** has an en-suite shower room and built-in double closets

- there is now **additional storage** in the new roof extension.

NEW LOFT LAYOUT

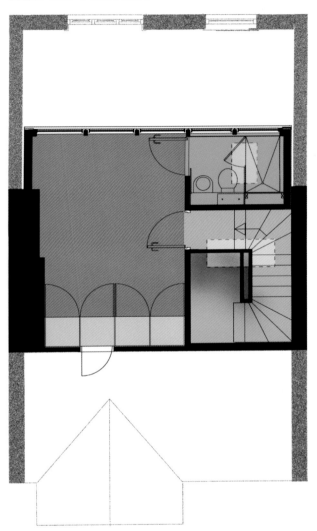

KEY

	BATHROOM
	EN-SUITE
	MASTER BEDROOM
	OTHER BEDROOMS
	HALLWAY
	STORAGE

0   5M

How about sharing a first home

Another option to consider for this modernized 'two up, two down' property would involve creating spaces that work for two sharers starting out on the property ladder – rather than a growing family.

To create a sense of space and privacy, the first floor could turn into two bedrooms, both with en-suite facilities, rather than three bedrooms sharing one bathroom.

This would then allow the roof extension to become a study and home cinema, rather than a master bedroom with en-suite shower room. A sofa bed could be included for occasional guests – although a sofa bed on the ground floor would be more practical for using the downstairs toilet.

Obviously, the shower room facility could be maintained in the roof extension, albeit that the study and home cinema would be reduced in size. Or the room could return to its original intended use of bedroom and shower room, turning the property into a three-bedroom, three-bathroom house for three sharers.

OPTIONAL FIRST FLOOR LAYOUT

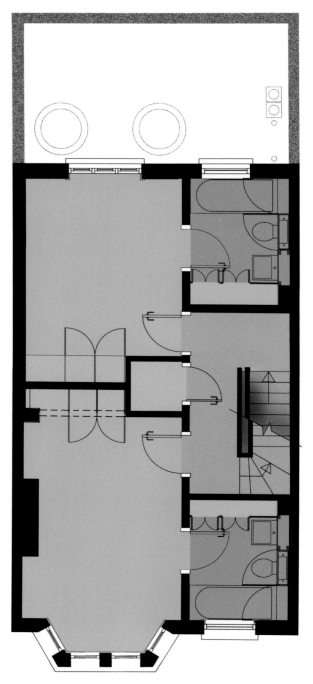

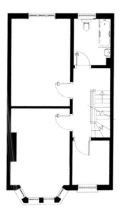

ORIGINAL FIRST FLOOR PLAN

■ the first floor communal bathroom becomes an en-suite **bathroom** for:
  – **bedroom 3** with built-in closets

■ **bedroom 2** – also with built-in closets – has a door into former bedroom 4, which becomes:
  – the **en-suite bathroom** for bedroom 2, instead of the smallest bedroom in the house

■ the master bedroom and en-suite shower room become the **study** and **home cinema**, ideal for professional sharers

■ each sharer has their own bedroom and bathroom, plus option of separate entertaining spaces. There would be a choice between the living room and kitchen/breakfast room on the ground floor, and the study/home cinema on the top floor

■ a sofa bed on the ground floor or top floor could accommodate occasional guests

OPTIONAL LOFT LAYOUT

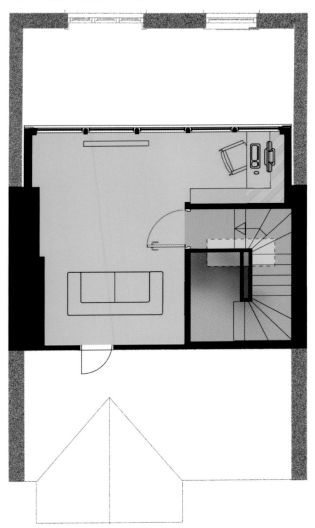

KEY

EN-SUITE

BEDROOM

HALLWAY

STORAGE

STUDY/HOME CINEMA

0   5M

1970s mish-mash to stylish one-bedroom apartment

DESIGNER: PAULA ROBINSON

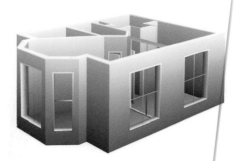

This property was originally the elegant main reception room of a large detached Victorian house. In the 1970s, the 34-square-metre reception room was converted into a practical, if somewhat clumsy, studio. The studio consisted of a corridor with built-in closets, a bathroom, steps leading up to a sleeping gallery above the bathroom, an open-plan reception room and extensive kitchen.

Existing problems

- the **corridor** was narrow and dark, flanked by closets

- the **bathroom** had a claustrophobically low ceiling

- the **sleeping gallery** was small and impossible to stand upright on

- the **reception area** was spacious and light, but dominated by:
  - a **kitchen** that was proportionally too large for the apartment and dominated the space

- minimal **storage space** was available – a particular problem in such a small apartment

Objectives

- to change the configuration from a studio into a one-bedroom apartment to increase the value of the property and make the space more versatile

- to create maximum storage space

- to replace the 'dark and dated' look with 'light and airy' to tie in with the high ceilings and maximum daylight

- to maintain the period features: 3.4m high ceilings, original cornicing and deep skirting boards

- to make maximum use of the large expanse of windows and south-west-facing aspect

ORIGINAL LAYOUT

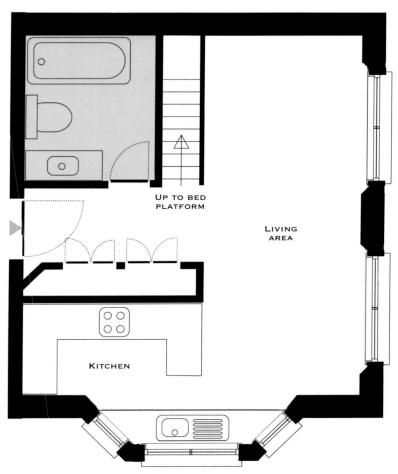

UP TO BED
PLATFORM

LIVING
AREA

KITCHEN

ORIGINAL MEZZANINE
BEDROOM SITUATED
ABOVE BATHROOM

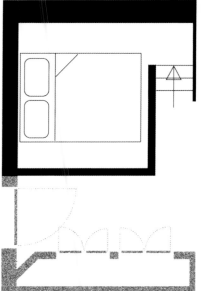

A possible split level solution

The apartment's 3.4-metre ceiling height put a lot of restrictions on finding a design solution that maximized the sense of space and light. Having liveable space on a raised level was the ideal, but this meant that anything below the raised area could only be used for storage – as there would not be sufficient head height to turn the lower area into liveable space.

The first design solution proposed having the bathroom and part of the bedroom on raised levels, storage underneath each of these areas, and a large open-plan reception room with discreet kitchen. A floor-to-ceiling glass wall between the reception room and the bedroom would add to the sense of space and light.

ORIGINAL FLOOR PLAN
KEY

■	BATHROOM
■	BEDROOM
■	HALLWAY
■	KITCHEN
■	LOUNGE
■	STORAGE

■ the **entrance hall** would give access to storage of 1.2m high below the bathroom and of 1.4m high below the raised portion of the bedroom. A washing machine and tumble dryer would be built into the latter space. Both storage areas would be tailored to the exact requirements of the owner and would be designed so that no space went to waste

■ the **bathroom**, with 2.1m head height, would be accessible via a half-spiral staircase from the reception area. Two glazed panels would allow daylight to filter into the bathroom

■ the **kitchen** immediately below the half-spiral staircase would be designed to be practical, discreet and to blend into the feel of:
  – the **reception room,** which would benefit from the full 3.4m ceiling height and two large windows. The sense of space would be enhanced by installing a floor-to-ceiling glass wall – with elegant, antique double doors in the centre of the wall – between the reception room and:
  – the **bedroom,** which would present on two levels. On ground level a dressing area with closets, on the mezzanine level a bed platform with 1.9m head height – thus contributing to the sense of space and light when sitting on the bed

■ the **glass wall** would be used instead of a standard partition wall to make the bedroom feel less claustrophobic. Privacy would be afforded either by using Privalite glass, which goes from clear to opaque at the flick of a switch, or by the more cost-effective solution of full-length muslin curtains

A CONSIDERED LAYOUT

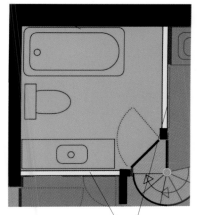

MEZZANINE BATHROOM

GLAZED AREAS TO ALLOW NATURAL LIGHT INTO THE BATHROOM

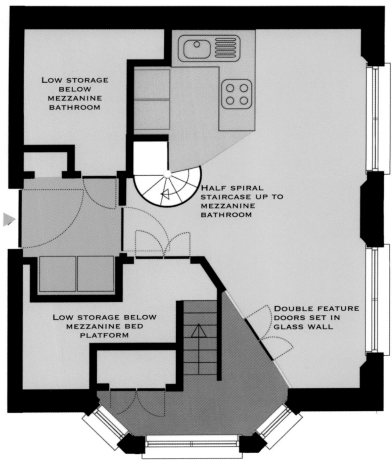

LOW STORAGE BELOW MEZZANINE BATHROOM

HALF SPIRAL STAIRCASE UP TO MEZZANINE BATHROOM

DOUBLE FEATURE DOORS SET IN GLASS WALL

LOW STORAGE BELOW MEZZANINE BED PLATFORM

MEZZANINE BED PLATFORM

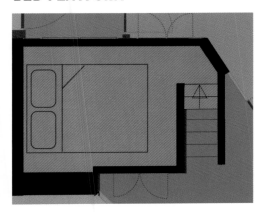

0   5M

The way the chosen option materialised

The second design solution reversed the levels: all living space now presents at ground level, with maximum storage space at high level.

The concept of the floor-to-ceiling glass wall to divide the bedroom and reception room was maintained, as was the idea of elegant double doors. Only this time one door opens into the reception room and the other into the bedroom. When both doors are closed, the impression from the hallway is of double doors leading to one room.

ORIGINAL FLOOR PLAN

KEY

	BATHROOM
	BEDROOM
	HALLWAY
	KITCHEN
	LOUNGE
	STORAGE
	WINDOWS/GLASS

- the **entrance hall** is somewhat larger than ideal for the flat's square footage, but is necessary to comply with Fire Regulations

- the **bathroom** was designed in a triangular shape in order to include a bath – an important feature for resale purposes. The bathroom has full-height storage concealed behind large antique French windows, adding an unusual feature

- the **kitchen**, despite its size, has all the amenities – oven, hob, washing machine, tumble dryer, dishwasher, fridge-freezer. Full-height storage is provided by glass-fronted cabinets that make the space practical, and appear larger than it really is

- the **reception room** combines storage needs with seating requirements and a home office. The bay window houses a built-in U-shaped seating area with storage below, and a rise and fall mechanized workstation that disappears at the touch of a button. A glass wall divides the reception room from:
  - the **bedroom,** which has floor-to-ceiling closets that double as the dividing wall between the bedroom and kitchen, giving excellent soundproofing

- the **glass wall** is 12mm thick and therefore very soundproof. Privacy is afforded between the bedroom and reception room by full-length muslin curtains, as the budget could not stretch to Privalite glass – which goes from clear to opaque at the flick of a switch

THE CHOSEN
LAYOUT

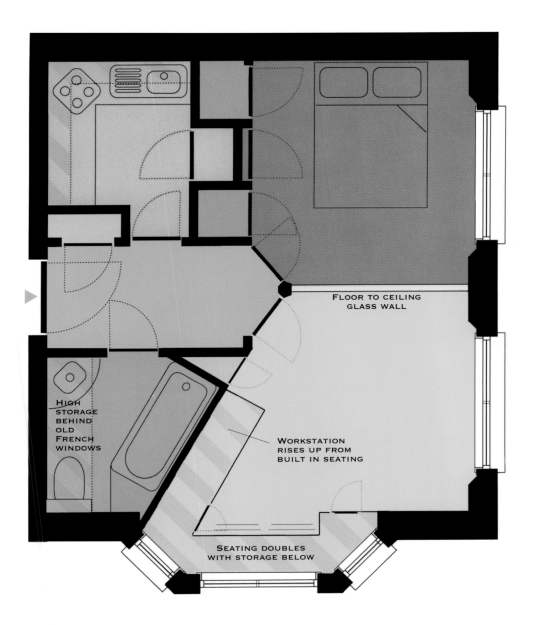

FLOOR TO CEILING
GLASS WALL

HIGH
STORAGE
BEHIND
OLD
FRENCH
WINDOWS

WORKSTATION
RISES UP FROM
BUILT IN SEATING

SEATING DOUBLES
WITH STORAGE BELOW

0   5M

From one century to the next – our changing requirements

CONCEPT: PAULA ROBINSON DESIGN GROUP

This detached property was originally built in the early 1900s in the middle of a large open field. Its idyllic setting belied the significant amount of work that needed to be carried out in order to bring the house from the last century firmly into present times. Meeting the very different needs of modern living would be essential in order to increase both the property's saleability and value.

The house presented on two poorly laid-out floors. The ground floor had a large living room and a small separate dining room. A long, dark passage then led to a very strange configuration. A large breakfast room (including an Aga) led directly into a comparatively small scullery/kitchen. A toilet, a tiny walk-in store room/pantry and a door leading to the garden completed the outdated ground floor layout. On the first floor, a master bedroom and three further bedrooms all shared one very small bathroom. Bedroom 4 was only large enough for a single bed.

Existing problems

- the layout was old-fashioned and impractical for modern living

- the **dining room** was an unnecessary requirement for a house that already had:
  - a **breakfast room** that was disproportionate in size to the **scullery/kitchen**. The presence of the Aga in the **breakfast room** would suggest that this area had originally been used as the kitchen

- the **corridor** and **store room/pantry** were a waste of space

- the **master bedroom** had no en-suite bathroom

- one small **bathroom** served all four bedrooms

Objectives

- to reconfigure both floors to make maximum use of available space

ORIGINAL FLOOR PLANS

GROUND FLOOR

TOILET

BREAKFAST ROOM

SCULLERY/ KITCHEN

STORE

FIRST FLOOR

LOUNGE

DINING ROOM

BATHROOM

BED 3

BED 4

MASTER BED

BED 2

- to completely modernize the property

- to introduce a utility room

- to create an en-suite facility for the master bedroom and a separate bathroom for the other bedrooms

- to create a contemporary home that would be at once practical, easy to live in and more valuable on the market

A floor redefined to reflect the blurring between rural and city life

The reconfiguration of the property addresses the very different needs of contemporary living. The ground floor has been turned into two separate open-plan living spaces. The dividing wall between the former living room and dining room has been demolished, a structural beam to support the upper floor put in place, and floor-to-ceiling folding doors installed between the two rooms. The living room is for formal entertaining and can be turned into a larger room by folding back the dividing doors. The former dining room, when not in use as an enlarged reception room, is a small media room.

Replacing the former maze of kitchen/scullery/breakfast room is a large open plan kitchen/dining area, with a separate utility room off the dining area.

ORIGINAL GROUND FLOOR PLAN

KEY

BATHROOM

HALLWAY

KITCHEN

LIVING AREA

STORAGE

UTILITY ROOM

- the **staircase** has been reconfigured and opened up to form a full-height gallery over the large spacious hallway below

- the **hallway** is now open and airy in feel, having lost the long dark corridor to the former breakfast area and toilet, and gained light from the gallery above

- the **living room** remains in its former location, but can open up into a double reception room thanks to double doors leading to:
  - the **media room,** which was formerly the dining room. The room works well both as part of an extended living room and as a cosy, separate media room. It includes a sofa bed so that it can easily be turned into a guest room if required

- the large, open-plan **kitchen/breakfast room** occupies what used to be the breakfast room, toilet and part of the long corridor. The former wall between the breakfast room and toilet has been completely removed, and a structural beam supports the floor above. The new kitchen/breakfast room now opens directly out onto the garden

- a separate **utility room** is accessed via the breakfast room

- a separate **toilet** opens out onto the main hallway

- two **closets** give practical storage on either side of the entrance to the kitchen/breakfast area

**REVISED GROUND
FLOOR LAYOUT**

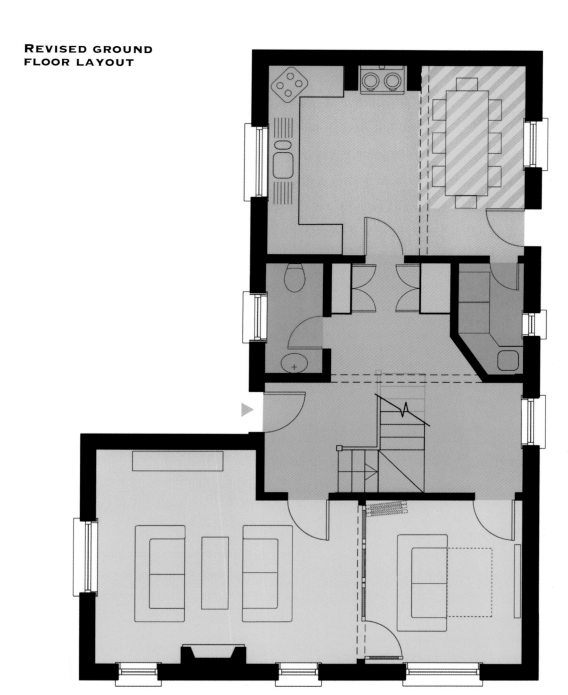

0   5M

Luxury living space still caters for modern 'average' family

The reconfigured first floor reduces the bedroom count from four to three, but adds an essential extra bathroom to the property. The master bedroom remains in its original position but now has built-in closets and a door leading into a large en-suite bathroom with separate shower. The new position of the staircase has allowed the creation of a second bathroom in an area that was formerly part of the landing and bedroom 4. Former bedroom 3 now includes built-in closets and a new entrance. The former bathroom – and part of the corridor – has become a single bedroom with built-in closets and two windows.

ORIGINAL FIRST FLOOR PLAN

KEY

	BATHROOM
	EN-SUITE
	MASTER BEDROOM
	OTHER BEDROOMS
	HALLWAY
	STORAGE

- the first floor **landing** benefits from an enlarged window that floods light down to the ground floor thanks to the galleried style staircase

- the **master bedroom** remains in its original position with 3 windows and a fireplace, but with the addition of built-in closets and double doors to:
  - the **en-suite bathroom** that replaces former bedroom 2. The new bathroom includes a double basin vanity unit, a separate shower and a large bath centred on the window

- former bedroom 3 now becomes **bedroom 2,** with a new entrance and built-in double closets. For a family with children, this bedroom could have bunk beds instead of a double bed

- **bedroom 3** is sited where the small communal bathroom was originally located. Bedroom 3 is only large enough for a single bed, or alternatively bunk beds. It has built-in closets

- the family **bathroom** occupies what used to be the landing for the first floor and part of former bedroom 4. It has a bath with overhead shower and a built-in vanity unit

- the loss of the fourth bedroom is compensated for by a **sofa bed** in the second reception room/media room on the ground floor. Whilst not ideal for long-term accommodation, as the media room does not have built-in closets, it is fine for short-term use

**REVISED FIRST
FLOOR LAYOUT**

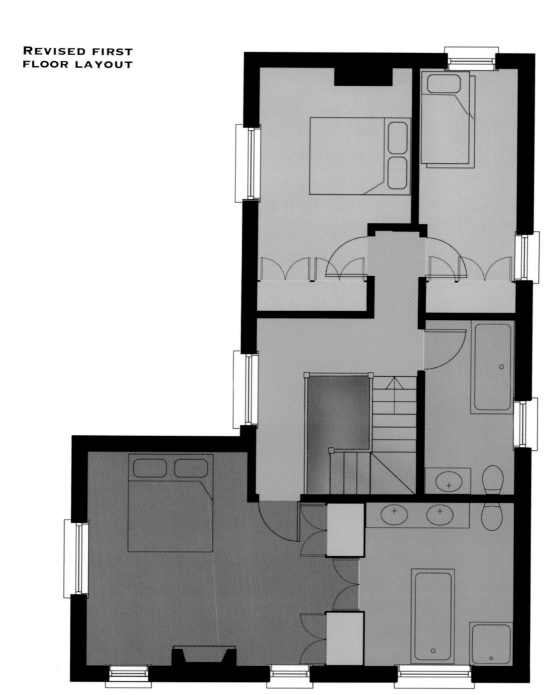

0   5M

A first-floor airy bachelor pad

ARCHITECT: JONATHAN CLARK

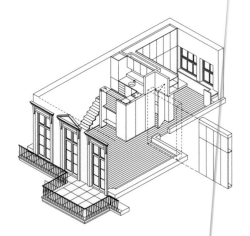

When this apartment was purchased in an unmodernized state, its features had been camouflaged. The impressive 3.65-metre ceilings were hidden behind suspended ceilings, making the apartment feel dark and cramped. The only room that felt light and somewhat airy was the living room/kitchen with its three large south-facing French windows – leading directly onto a full-width balcony/terrace. By contrast, the bathroom had no natural daylight, and the bedroom was small and box-like.

The apartment needed a new lease of life. It was essential to make it appear larger than it actually was, bringing a sense of flow to a space that was currently claustrophobic and chopped up.

Existing problems

■ the apartment lacked character and felt small

■ the **entrance corridor** had too many doors, contributing to a rabbit warren effect

■ the **living room** and **kitchen** were the only areas benefiting from any sense of light

■ the **bathroom** was small and had no natural light

■ the **bedroom** was small and uninteresting

Objectives

■ to remove the suspended ceilings and maximize the amount of available light

■ to increase the feeling of space in the apartment

■ to re-invent the space but using, as far as possible, the original footprint to minimize disruption to the main fabric of the building

ORIGINAL FLOOR PLAN

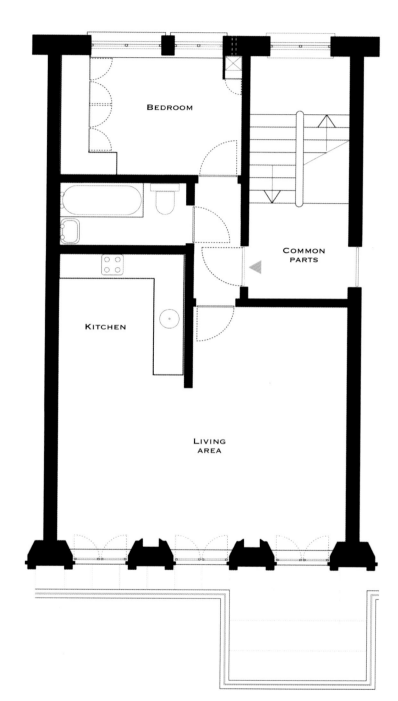

BEDROOM

COMMON PARTS

KITCHEN

LIVING AREA

■ to minimize the number of doors and the boxy feeling of the apartment

■ to create clean, uninterrupted lines, allowing surfaces and planes to flow and slide past each other

■ to create new storage space

Creating the illusion of space

The suspended ceilings and all of the existing walls were removed, but the position of both the bathroom and kitchen were maintained in an effort to reduce costs.

The kitchen was raised up by 1.4 metres to provide separation between it and the living room, while still maintaining the open-plan feel. The space below the kitchen was used for crawl-in storage.

In the bedroom, a storage platform sits over the top of the 2.2-metre ceiling of the bathroom. The bedroom ceiling therefore flows over the bathroom ceiling, giving an added sense of dimension.

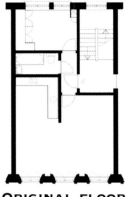

ORIGINAL FLOOR PLAN

- the **entrance corridor** doors have been reduced in number

- the **kitchen** has been raised up by 1.4m to give an illusion of additional space without losing the open plan feel. The sinks can be covered with flush stainless steel lids to create additional work surfaces when required

- crawl-in **storage** has been created under the kitchen platform

- the **bedroom** has been given the optical illusion of additional space by creating a storage platform over the top of the 2.2m bathroom ceiling

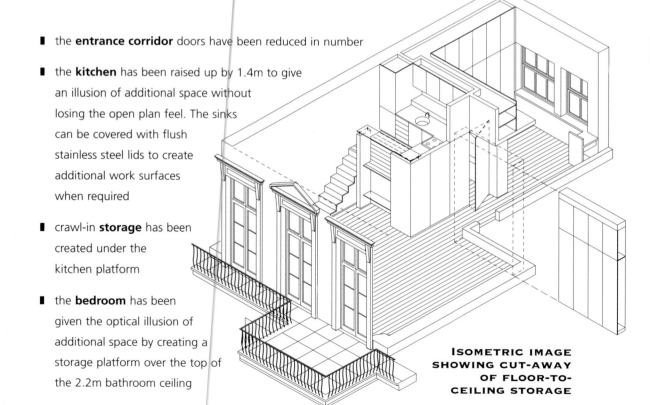

ISOMETRIC IMAGE SHOWING CUT-AWAY OF FLOOR-TO-CEILING STORAGE

GROUND LEVEL LAYOUT

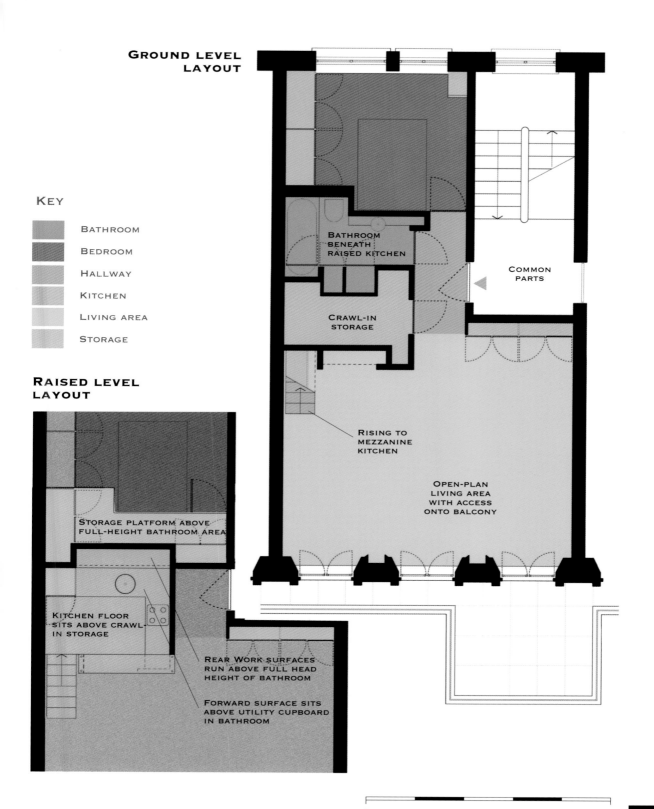

KEY

- BATHROOM
- BEDROOM
- HALLWAY
- KITCHEN
- LIVING AREA
- STORAGE

RAISED LEVEL LAYOUT

BATHROOM BENEATH RAISED KITCHEN

COMMON PARTS

CRAWL-IN STORAGE

RISING TO MEZZANINE KITCHEN

OPEN-PLAN LIVING AREA WITH ACCESS ONTO BALCONY

STORAGE PLATFORM ABOVE FULL-HEIGHT BATHROOM AREA

KITCHEN FLOOR SITS ABOVE CRAWL IN STORAGE

REAR WORK SURFACES RUN ABOVE FULL HEAD HEIGHT OF BATHROOM

FORWARD SURFACE SITS ABOVE UTILITY CUPBOARD IN BATHROOM

0   5M

Turning a 1960s site into contemporary living space

ARCHITECT: SPENCE HARRIS HOGAN

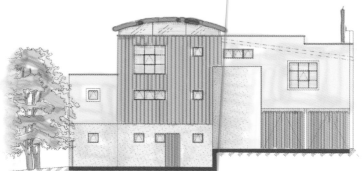

A split-level 1960s building with two floors was stripped back to the shell then, with the addition of a side extension and third level, reconfigured into a contemporary four/five bedroom family house. The main emphasis of the project was to increase the value of the property.

The new house is a play on levels and overlapping spaces, with a central staircase linking all the floors. This has a full height internal window, allowing maximum visibility and overlap between the living and dining areas on the split levels.

The lower ground floor is suited to older children, a live-in nanny or guests, who would have the use of their own utility room/small kitchen.

- the **entrance** is to the side of the house onto a large half-landing located between the lower ground and upper ground floors. It is on the same level as the garage

- a long **corridor** leads to bedrooms 2, 3 and 4 and their bathrooms, and a recreation room/bedroom 5

- **bedroom 4** is a single bedroom with a large window overlooking the garden

- **bedroom 3** is a double bedroom with a storage wall and built-in closet shared with bedroom 4. It also overlooks the garden, and has large double doors out onto the raised decking area

- **bathroom 3** faces the front of the house

- a **utility room/small kitchen** is sited between the floor's two bathrooms and is designed for potential live-in nanny use or teenage children

- **bedroom 2,** with its **en-suite bathroom,** faces the front of the house

LOWER GROUND FLOOR

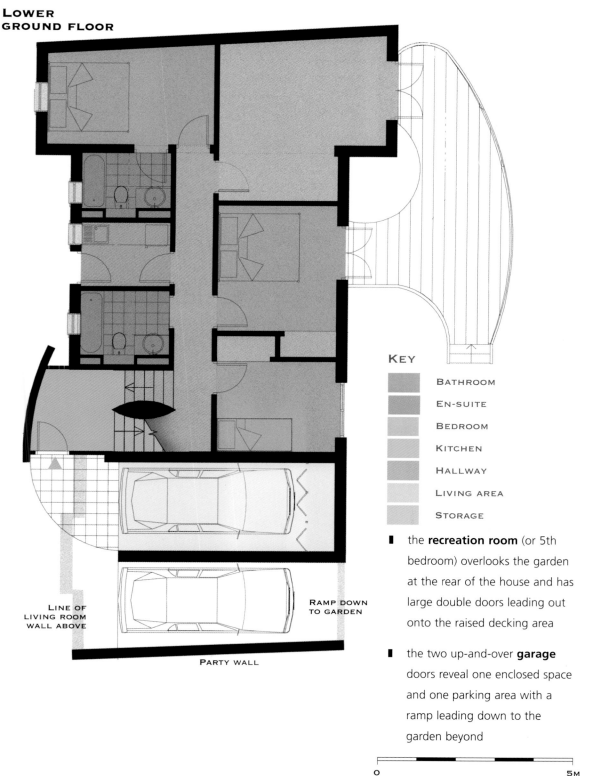

LINE OF
LIVING ROOM
WALL ABOVE

RAMP DOWN
TO GARDEN

PARTY WALL

KEY

- BATHROOM
- EN-SUITE
- BEDROOM
- KITCHEN
- HALLWAY
- LIVING AREA
- STORAGE

■ the **recreation room** (or 5th bedroom) overlooks the garden at the rear of the house and has large double doors leading out onto the raised decking area

■ the two up-and-over **garage** doors reveal one enclosed space and one parking area with a ramp leading down to the garden beyond

0   5M

Maximum entertaining space on multiple levels

The staircase leads up to the ground floor, with views through glass straight into the large dining room overlooking the garden. The glass adds to the spacious, light feel of the space and brings further natural light to the corridor and stairs. Within the dining room, steps lead up directly into the raised level living area, which extends across the width of the house. A huge picture window throws light onto the steps linking the two entertaining levels.

Back on ground level, a corridor leads to the large open-plan kitchen and breakfast room complete with skylight doors leading out onto a terrace. A shower room, utility room and built-in closet complete the ground floor.

KEY

- BATHROOM
- HALLWAY
- KITCHEN
- LIVING AREA
- STORAGE
- UTILITY ROOM

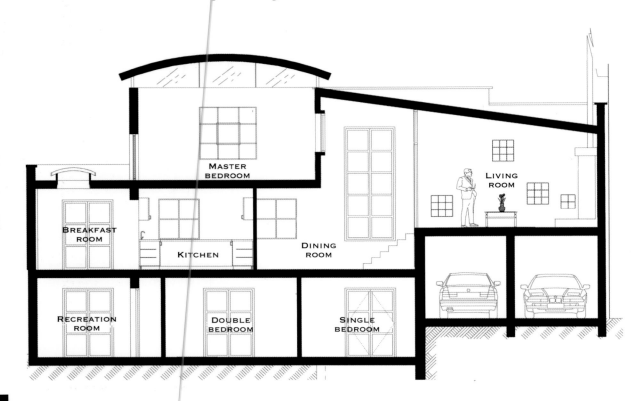

MASTER BEDROOM

BREAKFAST ROOM

KITCHEN

DINING ROOM

LIVING ROOM

RECREATION ROOM

DOUBLE BEDROOM

SINGLE BEDROOM

UPPER GROUND FLOOR LAYOUT

▌ the **staircase** has a void over the entrance area, adding to the sense of space and light

▌ the **dining room** is immediately visible from the main staircase leading to the upper levels, as a glazed wall brings light into the stairwell and corridor. The garden beyond is also visible through a full-height picture window positioned on the outside wall, immediately opposite the dining room's glazed wall onto the landing

▌ the **living room** is also accessed via steps from the dining room. It has an unusual configuration of windows on the garden side and a large single window on the front of the house. The open-plan layout between the dining room and living room on split levels gives a sense of space, height and volume

▌ the open-plan **kitchen** with skylight opens into the spacious breakfast room and onto a terrace that overlooks the garden

▌ the **shower room** serves the entertaining level of the house and opens into the utility room

▌ the built-in **closet** completes the floor plan

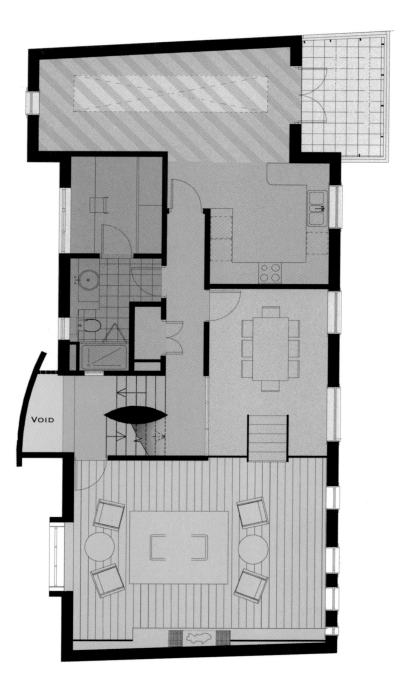

Void

0   5M

A master suite of privacy

The exterior of the building was completely re-rendered and re-clad in Western red cedar – also used for all the house windows – fulfilling conservation area regulations and echoing the original construction. The final material in the external materials palette was copper, used for a new barrel-vaulted roof, below which the master bedroom sits, with a sub-dividing dwarf wall for a bathroom and walk-in closet.

This master bedroom sits in splendid isolation on the first floor, nicely cut off from the hustle and bustle of the floors below. To the rear and one side, it has views onto the garden; from the other side it overlooks the lounge and dining room. The large en-suite bathroom is accessed from two sides via sliding doors and faces the front of the property.

KEY

En-suite

Master bedroom

Hallway

Storage

REAR ELEVATION

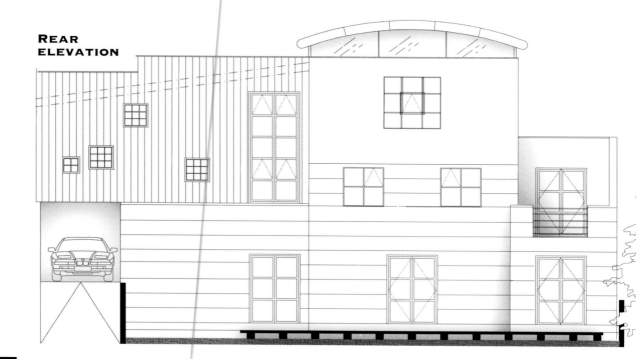

FIRST FLOOR LAYOUT

▮ the staircase leads up to the first floor and its self-contained master suite

▮ the **master bedroom** overlooks the garden and is a large, uncluttered space that centres around the bed placed immediately opposite the huge window for maximum views. A second window to the side brings yet more light

▮ the **en-suite bathroom** is designed to be either open-plan to the bedroom, or separate. Two separate entrances lead to the bathroom via sliding doors that are left open for open-plan mode and closed for a sense of separation. The bathroom includes double-basin vanity unit, a bath, a separate shower and a separate toilet accessed via a sliding door for added privacy. Built-in closets stand at opposite ends of the bathroom, providing his-and-hers dressing areas. The bathroom has a very large window overlooking the front of the house and bringing maximum light. The toilet has a small window to avoid any sense of being too enclosed

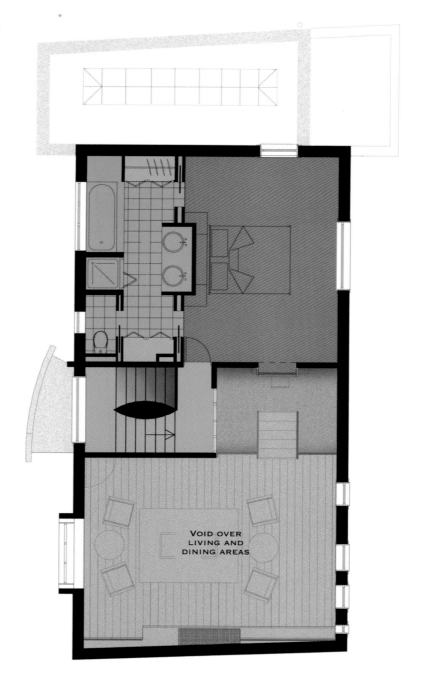

VOID OVER LIVING AND DINING AREAS

0   5M

Finding an en-suite solution for a seven-bedroom house

CONCEPT: PAULA ROBINSON DESIGN GROUP

One of the many requirements for a high-value multi-bedroom house is that the master bedroom, at the very least, should benefit from an en-suite bathroom.

This seven-bedroom suburban house was arranged over four floors, which included bedroom 2 on the lower ground floor with a separate bathroom. Extensive works had already been carried out on the lower two floors, raising the standards of this fine home. The subject of this reconfiguration concept applies only to the upper floors.

The house is large enough to redevelop into separate apartments. Therefore any works carried out on it as a whole house must add to its overall resale value and appeal as one property.

Existing problems

- a high proportion of bedrooms compared to bathrooms

- a master bedroom that did not benefit from en-suite facilities, but instead shared a bathroom with two other large bedrooms on the same floor

- achieving a good price on resale would be doubtful without an en-suite facility

Objectives

- to transform the space to include a master suite with en-suite bathroom

- any further transformation must not compromise the value of the property

- a close eye would need to be kept on building costs to ensure that they could be recouped in the added value of the property

ORIGINAL FLOOR PLANS

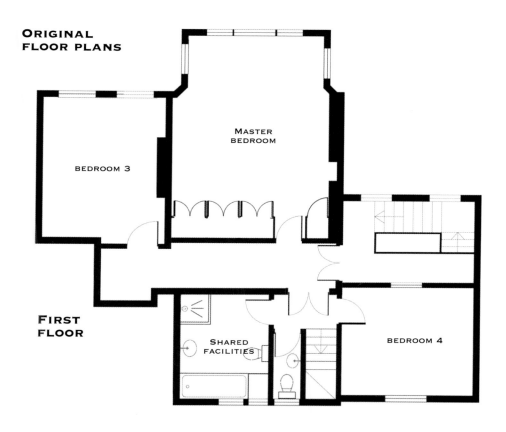

BEDROOM 3

MASTER BEDROOM

FIRST FLOOR

SHARED FACILITIES

BEDROOM 4

SECOND FLOOR

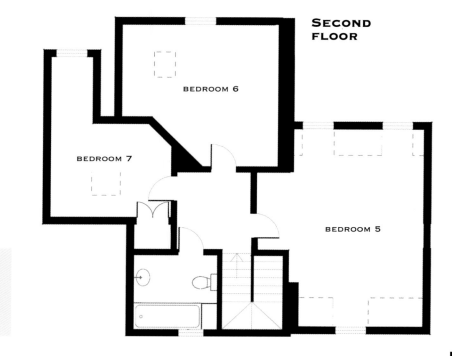

BEDROOM 6

BEDROOM 7

BEDROOM 5

AS THIS CONCEPT RELATES TO THE TOP TWO FLOORS, ONLY THESE FLOOR PLANS ARE SHOWN.

The obvious solution may not always be the best

The most common way of creating an en-suite is to annex an adjoining room – in this case bedroom 3 – and fit it out as a bathroom. Three options for this property, and their disadvantages, are shown below.

ORIGINAL FIRST FLOOR PLAN

KEY

	BATHROOM
	EN-SUITE
	DRESSING AREA
	MASTER BEDROOM
	OTHER BEDROOMS
	HALLWAY

OPTION 1

▮ knock a door through to the adjacent room, which becomes the new en-suite bathroom

▮ close up the doorway to the main corridor – to achieve privacy

▮ this involves a minimum of structural work

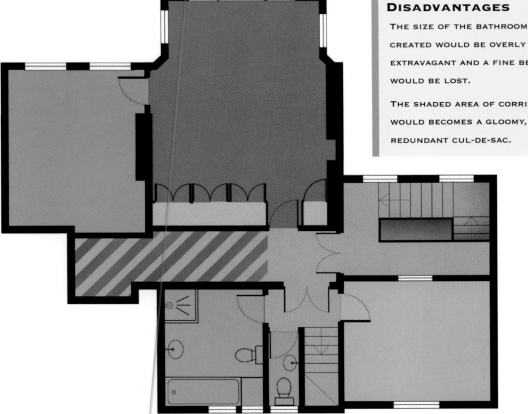

DISADVANTAGES

THE SIZE OF THE BATHROOM CREATED WOULD BE OVERLY EXTRAVAGANT AND A FINE BEDROOM WOULD BE LOST.

THE SHADED AREA OF CORRIDOR WOULD BECOMES A GLOOMY, REDUNDANT CUL-DE-SAC.

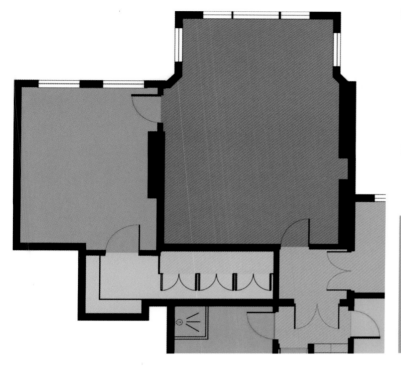

OPTION 2

- identical to option 1 except that it retains the original door to bedroom 3 and makes use of the redundant corridor as a walk-in closet/dressing room

- this removes the built-in closets from the master bedroom, giving a maximum sense of space

DISADVANTAGE

THE RESULTING DRESSING AREA WOULD NOT OFFER SUFFICIENTLY COMFORTABLE STORAGE AND CIRCULATING SPACE OR NATURAL LIGHT TO MAKE THE SOLUTION WORTHWHILE

OPTION 3

- this option includes the dressing area/closets within the master suite itself, thereby maximizing light to the area – an issue for option 2

- the master bedroom retains its spaciousness but could feel awkward in terms of shape

DISADVANTAGES

EXPENSIVE: SUBSTANTIAL STRUCTURAL SUPPORT IN PLACE OF THE REMOVED WALL, NEW FLOOR COVERING AND CEILING REPAIRS WOULD BE REQUIRED

RESULTING BEDROOM WOULD BE AN AWKWARD SHAPE

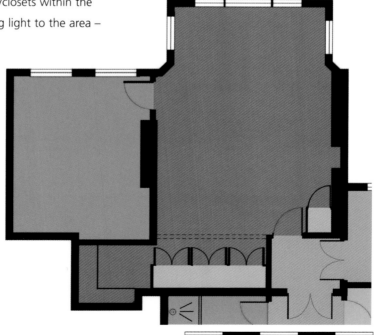

0   5M

Overlaying the floor plans reveals a unique solution

A better solution would be to look to the floor above and choose one of the smallest and least practical bedrooms in terms of both floor space and head height. Bedroom 7, with its single dormer window, would be a perfect size for a master bathroom. Better still, it is positioned immediately above bedroom 3 and its access corridor, with part of its awkward shape immediately above the master bedroom itself. A spiral staircase rising from the master bedroom to the floor above would be the way towards creating an en-suite bathroom.

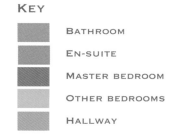

KEY

- BATHROOM
- EN-SUITE
- MASTER BEDROOM
- OTHER BEDROOMS
- HALLWAY

FIRST AND SECOND FLOOR PLANS SUPERIMPOSED

■ the second floor plan is shown superimposed over the first floor plan (in brown). The overlapping area (in yellow) is ideal for accessing this room from the master bedroom below to create an en-suite bathroom above it

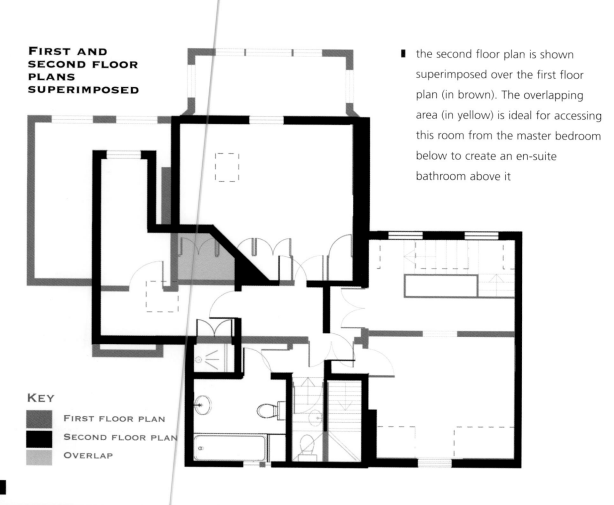

KEY

- FIRST FLOOR PLAN
- SECOND FLOOR PLAN
- OVERLAP

**CONCEPT FOR THE
NEW BATHROOM**

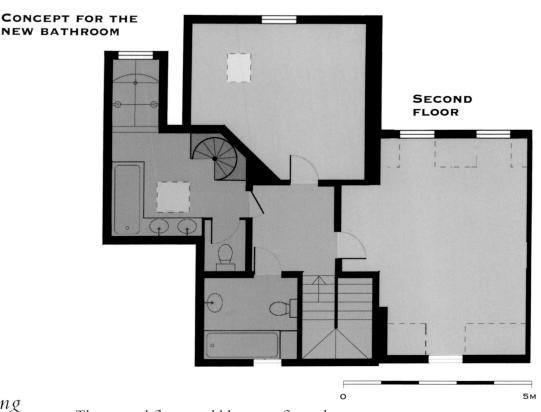

**SECOND
FLOOR**

0   5M

*Going
upwards
instead of
sideways*

The second floor could be reconfigured
with a spiral staircase rising through the
overlapping area between the floors. The
new master bathroom makes maximum use
of the awkward shapes on hand. The higher expense of this
solution would be more than outweighed by the novelty
factor, to the right type of buyer.

▌ a wet room has been created in the troublesome
rectangle by the dormer window

▌ the toilet takes up the second awkward rectangle
and has its own door for added privacy

▌ the only disadvantage to this two-level
configuration is the fact that a spiral staircase could
only be 1.2m in diameter. Although this is quite a

common width for a spiral, it is not the easiest
staircase to climb. Getting any large or bulky items
up or down the spiral would be difficult

▌ the original bedroom 7 door is retained – but hung
to open outwards – to aid access for repairs or
refurbishment. This could also serve as a secondary
means of escape in the event of fire

FLEXIBLE SPACE

*Movable partitions: spaces
that adapt to suit your mood*

*T*he notion of flexible space is still relatively new to us, but understanding the direction that our homes are headed in will help us to prepare for a new way of living.

As our lifestyles evolve and technology continues to facilitate our lives, our homes will become spaces that we can alter as the mood takes us. Within a fixed footprint, we will be able to open and close the internal spaces of our home, based on our personal requirement of the moment. Technology has ensured that key elements such as underfloor heating, ventilation, insulation and climate control are now under easy personal control.

Divisions of space can now be – or appear to be – as permanent or impermanent as we desire: blinds that drop out of their concealed ceiling positions, solid walls that slide back completely into other walls, movable glass walls that can be clear or opaque at the touch of a button, fabric divisions that change colour to suit. We are only at the start of flexible space division, and there are many more innovations to come.

Looking ahead

As we progress, a home's original construction will no longer define its layout. Instead, mood and practical considerations will be the defining factors.

When entertaining requires a large open area, divisions can be retracted to allow people free circulation. When a more cosy, secluded atmosphere is required, divisions can be reintroduced in a configuration to suit. Individual preference will govern whether an area is large or small, with change possible at the touch of a few buttons.

Working from the flexible home

Perhaps the biggest dilemma that we will face with flexible space division is how to accommodate working from home successfully. More and more people are having to tackle this issue, whether through personal choice or under corporate directive. Some welcome the opportunity, while others find it extremely difficult. Regardless of the reaction, the problems of transforming a home environment into an office-friendly zone are numerous.

Beyond the obvious issues of noise disruption from other family members or home-related tasks, there are some deeper psychological barriers to working from home that our new, flexible layouts need to address and overcome. One of the keys to successful flexible space is that the home becomes a chameleon, changing its identity to fit our needs. Anything that restricts us or hampers our movements means that the space cannot be deemed 'flexible'.

GETTING OVER HISTORY

A century of office-based work has not predisposed us to working from home. The ritual of getting up and commuting to work on weekdays – and looking forward to the luxury of being at home at the weekend – is taken as red by many of us.

While we often dread the commute to work, it's possible that the ritual of commuting prepares us for entering the work environment and performing appropriately. We have become accustomed to easing ourselves into the working day through commuting. The notion of jumping from our bed to our desk and switching instantaneously to work mode is alien to most of us.

Most successful home-workers find that establishing a routine to build up to the start of work is essential. And being able to cut off at the end of the working day is equally important.

In the past, the action of leaving the office went hand-in-glove with psychologically leaving work behind. Today, when the office is at home, the cut-off point is less well defined. Working erratic, longer hours is a frequent issue for the home-based, with the big temptation either to shirk or overwork.

LEAVING THE WORKROOM BEHIND

Until now, our model for working – like our model for eating – has been handed down to us through centuries of history. Both activities have traditionally taken place in a designated room, complete with hard, flat surface to sit at and chairs to sit on. The dining room has only recently lost its prominence in most homes. Many have been turned into home offices or opened up as extra living space, as more relaxed eating and entertaining patterns replace formal dining.

Work patterns have proved somewhat harder to break than eating habits. We tend to accept the current way of working, partly because it has been ingrained in us from a young age.

Back to the drawing board

To divide or to integrate? The most important decision is whether you actually want – or indeed need – a clear division between your living and working areas. If you do want boundaries between work and home, there are limited solutions. With the luxury of space, an entire room can be allocated to the office. Otherwise, a designated area can be created.

CONCEALING THE EVIDENCE OF WORK

When work is viewed as a separate entity from home life, it is essential that a sense of control over work be established.

A traditional desk or work surface is, for the most part, solid and immovable – except with considerable physical effort. It is possible to switch off the computer, put away all

paperwork and visible signs of the office, but you will still be faced with the working surface – an ominous tombstone, ever present and beckoning. What to do with it?

If a home office has to double as a bedroom, consider a wall unit with a central workstation. When guests arrive, the workstation slides effortlessly into one of the side units. The sofa bed is placed in the void. The workstation can still be accessed from its new position, by opening the doors of the side unit.

Concealing a workstation and office storage behind cupboard doors is a solution, but it has its drawbacks. Doors that slide, swing open, or even disappear into a wall to reveal an area crammed from floor to ceiling with the components of the office can be a daunting sight first thing in the morning. Does anyone really want to work in an oversized, open cupboard all day?

Although this is a practical solution for the spatially challenged, few of us produce our best work in conditions like these. Psychologically, this arrangement reminds us of a solid, impassable wall, with no room for manoeuvre. The shelving immediately above and to either side weighs heavily and threateningly.

To add further discomfort, the location of these sorts of units often requires us to sit with our back to the door, an instinctively disconcerting position. This huge monument to work fosters the sense that work controls us, which is not the objective.

SOLUTIONS THAT GIVE US CONTROL

Solutions that ensure a feeling of control over work often involve imagination and a sense of fun. A work area that rises up to reveal itself at the touch of a button may conjure up images of King Arthur and James Bond, but it also offers a greater psychological command over work. The work area then ceases to be oppressive and threatening in appearance, as its components no longer tower above us, heavy and looming.

Whether we are conscious of it or not, the appearance and layout of the spaces in which we live and work affect us and our behaviour profoundly. It is essential that the designated space should cater to every aspect of our work requirements. The office or work area demands as much thought, planning and indulgence of individualism as any other fixed area in the home, such as the kitchen and bathroom. Layout, colours, mood and atmosphere must tie in with both our personality and our line of work. These factors help to enforce a sense of control over work, since the latter is often seen as an intruder into private space.

BLENDING WORK INTO THE HOME

For those who do not feel the pressing need to segregate work and home, flexible space has a lot to offer.

The first question to ask yourself is whether it is absolutely essential for you to work at a desk or whether this is just what you are used to. If you do opt for a desk, does it need to be hard and uncomfortable or could it be a soft, comfortable surface?

Next, find your own ideal work spots and methods. Start with you and your needs. Don't feel compelled to conform to any previous or existing model; be flexible and make up your own.

TAKING A CUE FROM ARTISTS

Artists have always been adept at picking exactly the right spot to work in, creating an atmosphere around them that will be inspiring. The light and the need for a practical working space dictate their choice of work area. Convention does not even enter into the equation.

Sadly, corporate office life has deprived many of us of the instinctive sense of what our best working spot might be. The strict discipline of sitting at a desk has been enforced to a point where we no longer believe that we can be productive outside this rigid setting.

Going with the flow Whereas artists are extremely sensitive to light and its changing quality throughout the day, those of us who are used to working in offices frequently have no sense of these changes. Nevertheless, our bodies are still subject to the energy peaks and troughs that all humans experience daily.

Following the body's natural cyclical rhythms ensures better work output. Working from home opens up the possibility of pursuing a more natural pattern of work. Varying both light levels and working areas can be an important enabler for us, since contemplating the same objects in the same place, day in, day out, encourages stagnation of thought and action.

MOVING WORKSPACES

Since movement and change are crucial to many creative thinkers, working in different areas of the home at different times of the day can be very liberating. With the equipment and components of work becoming ever smaller and more mobile, working 'on the move' is easily achieved.

Technology also has an answer for those less inclined to move around themselves: consider a section of floor in a given space that actually moves, slowly and progressively during the course of a day. The pace, direction and configuration of movement and the area covered can be set to individual requirements – anything from keeping pace with the gradual movement of the sun across the room, to a more immediately discernible movement.

The concept can be viewed as an indulgence of childhood memories of merry-go-rounds or as another tool in building a sense of progress and accomplishment throughout the day.

VERSATILE FLOORS

Once you've decided on the configuration of your flexible space – whether it includes an area of moving floor or not – you need to turn your attention to the material of the flooring itself.

Carpeted flooring may offer luxury and softness, but hard floor coverings work best for flexible space. Where carpet will show the tell-tale signs of the previous position of a retractable partition, a hard floor covering will not.

With underfloor heating and occasional rugs, there is no reason for hard flooring to feel cold and uninviting.

A note of caution   Before you give yourself licence to knock down all your walls and create your flexible space, do be sure to make structural support your main priority. Consult a structural engineer or architect about your adventurous plans and pay close attention to their concerns.

Glass walls may be a wonderful idea and look amazing once installed, but the support required and the actual installation are a far cry from what is required for a standard plasterboard wall. Loads have to be calculated and additional support added. Apart from which, glass is also heavy and difficult to install.

A flexible mind   One of the keys to creating successful flexible space is to give your mind licence to be flexible. Letting go of old habits, beliefs and preconceptions is essential. Examining your needs and requirements and exploring the possibilities with as great a sense of freedom as possible will yield tremendous results.

Imagination and creativity have a great part to play in making flexible space that will work for you, not only now but also well into the future.

One space — triple usage

ARCHITECT: JONATHAN CLARK

This 88-square-metre first floor apartment had the advantage of being located in a beautiful, Grade II-listed, Victorian end-of-terrace house. It faced south-west and so benefited from maximum daylight. But the advantages stopped there. Previous internal reconfiguration had left the property with awkward accommodation, including inequitable room sizes and room locations that made little practical sense. Although the apartment was end-of-terrace, its centre was dark and gloomy.

Existing problems

- the **entrance** had a claustrophobic double lobby

- the **access corridor** was long, narrow and took up too great a percentage of the overall floor space of the apartment

- the **living room** was fundamentally well proportioned, but its entrance afforded neither privacy nor an open-plan feel. Instead it felt as if the living room door had been removed

- the **kitchen** was small, but not unacceptable in terms of position within the flat

- the **master bedroom** was badly positioned, being immediately next to both the apartment's entrance, and the open living room. This raised issues of privacy and soundproofing

- the **en-suite shower room** should, ideally, have been a bathroom instead. It also had no natural daylight

- **bathroom 2** was badly positioned in relation to the two bedrooms that it was meant to serve

- **bedroom 2** and **3**/or **study** were small and lacked built-in closets or workspace

- **dropped ceilings** further enclosed the overall space

ORIGINAL FLOOR PLAN

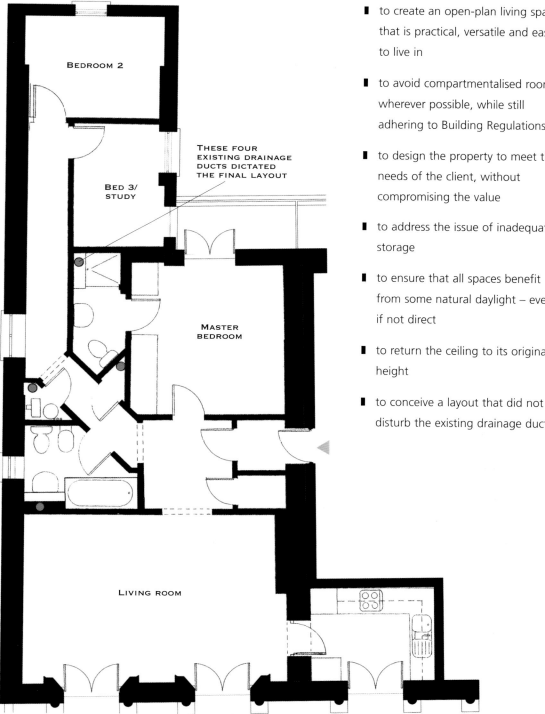

BEDROOM 2

THESE FOUR
EXISTING DRAINAGE
DUCTS DICTATED
THE FINAL LAYOUT

BED 3/
STUDY

MASTER
BEDROOM

LIVING ROOM

Objectives

▌ to create an open-plan living space that is practical, versatile and easy to live in

▌ to avoid compartmentalised rooms wherever possible, while still adhering to Building Regulations

▌ to design the property to meet the needs of the client, without compromising the value

▌ to address the issue of inadequate storage

▌ to ensure that all spaces benefit from some natural daylight – even if not direct

▌ to return the ceiling to its original height

▌ to conceive a layout that did not disturb the existing drainage ducts

All opened up for maximum light and space

All internal walls and dropped ceilings were removed from the property, and a new structural frame was inserted to support the four floors above. This allowed the apartment to become truly versatile and open-plan. The owners did not require three bedrooms, but instead wanted a maximum sense of space for everyday living. A second bedroom and a study were only occasional requirements, so these two areas could not form a fixed part of the permanent layout.

ORIGINAL FLOOR PLAN

The solution to the dilemma came in the form of a full-height, top-hung, sliding acoustic wall, housed discreetly in a recess in the dining section of the reception areas. This wall can be pulled out at will to divide the space to include a separate bedroom or study as required – as shown on the pages that follow.

- a completely **open-plan layout** was achieved by using extensive structural supports to the four floors above

- the **entrance lobby** has been simplified to make it practically unnoticeable while still complying with Building Regulations

- the **double reception area** is a zone of space and light. An etched glass panel gives a sense of privacy and separation between the reception room and corridor leading to the master suite

- **acoustic panels**, folded neatly away in the dining section of the reception area, can be closed to form either:
  - **bedroom 2** or
  - **study**

- the **kitchen** has also been opened up to the reception room, making it feel less restricted

- the **shower room** now benefits from natural daylight. It also transmits light to the corridor by means of an etched glass panel, without compromising privacy in the shower itself

- the **master suite** benefits from maximum light and includes a walk-in closet with daylight from its own window. Although the corridor to the master suite is long, the light distracts the eye, making it feel elegant. The master bedroom is now correctly located, far away from the main entrance and the reception room

- the **en-suite bathroom** now has natural daylight and a sleek and unusual layout

- **storage** has been created in the form of raised platforms over both of the bathrooms

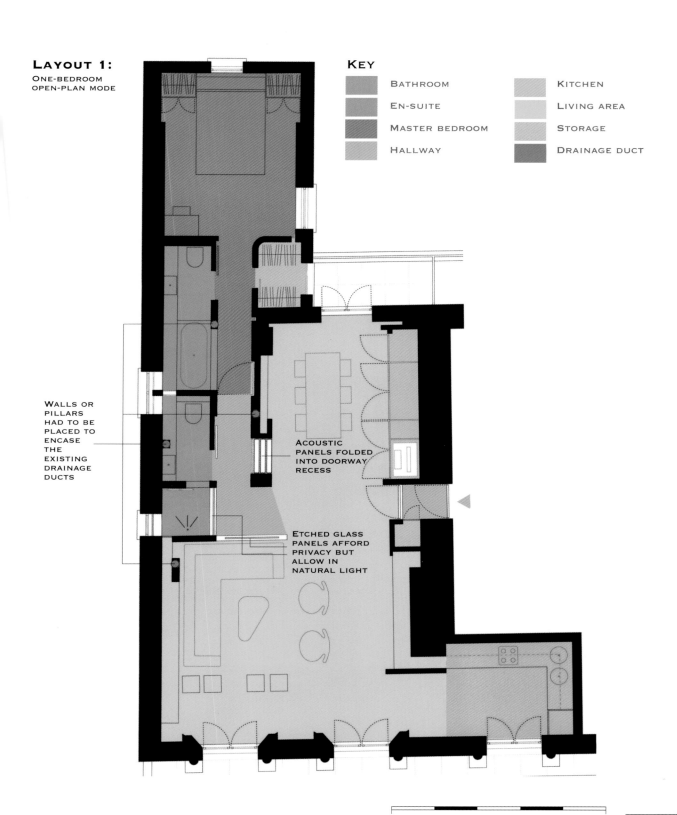

LAYOUT 1:

ONE-BEDROOM
OPEN-PLAN MODE

KEY

BATHROOM

EN-SUITE

MASTER BEDROOM

HALLWAY

KITCHEN

LIVING AREA

STORAGE

DRAINAGE DUCT

WALLS OR
PILLARS
HAD TO BE
PLACED TO
ENCASE
THE
EXISTING
DRAINAGE
DUCTS

ACOUSTIC
PANELS FOLDED
INTO DOORWAY
RECESS

ETCHED GLASS
PANELS AFFORD
PRIVACY BUT
ALLOW IN
NATURAL LIGHT

0   5M

103

Second bedroom in a flash

When guests appear, this one-bedroom apartment transforms itself into a two-bedroom apartment with minimal effort. The dining table is moved into the main section of the reception area. The acoustic panels fold out and divide what used to be the dining section of the reception room into a private second bedroom – complete with its own door immediately opposite the guest bathroom.

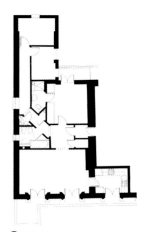

ORIGINAL FLOOR PLAN

LAYOUT 2:
TWO BEDROOM MODE

DOORWAY IN USE ONLY IN THIS MODE

- the **entrance** and **corridor** become more defined and less open-plan in feel because of the presence of the acoustic wall. The etched glass panel of the shower wall comes into its own here, bringing daylight into the corridor

- the **reception room** is no longer double but single, and also has to accommodate the dining table and chairs. The only drawback is the tight circulating space with the dining table in this position

- the **kitchen** is unchanged

- the **second bedroom** is self-contained, private and spacious. A double bed pulls down from a wall panel

- the **guest bathroom** is unchanged

- the **master suite** is unchanged

Or even a home office When guests are not around but work beckons, the acoustic wall remains in its original concealed position, the guest bed folds back up into its wall panel, the dining table remains in the reception room, and a versatile workstation pulls out from the wall storage unit to create the home office.

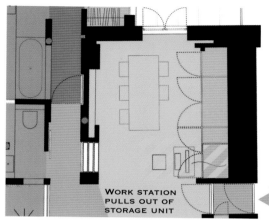

LAYOUT 3:
HOME-OFFICE MODE

WORK STATION
PULLS OUT OF
STORAGE UNIT

0   5M

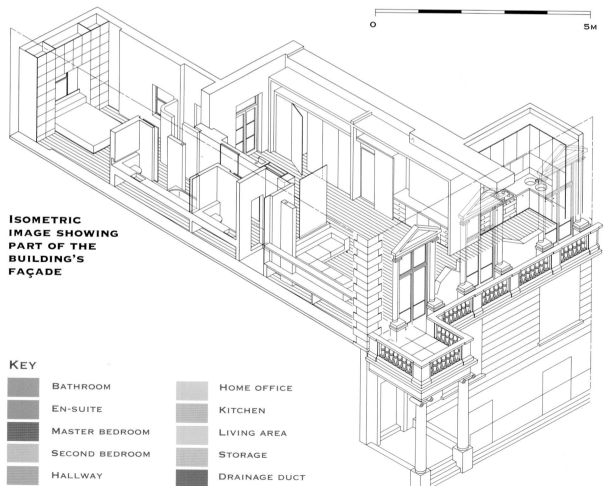

ISOMETRIC IMAGE SHOWING PART OF THE BUILDING'S FAÇADE

KEY

	BATHROOM		HOME OFFICE
	EN-SUITE		KITCHEN
	MASTER BEDROOM		LIVING AREA
	SECOND BEDROOM		STORAGE
	HALLWAY		DRAINAGE DUCT

Flexible loft-style space and roof terrace extension

DESIGNER: PAULA ROBINSON DESIGN GROUP

This period building had the advantage of being sited on top of a hill, which gave this fourth-floor apartment panoramic views, especially from the extensive roof terrace. The apartment's original arrangement included an open-plan reception room, two small bedrooms, a bathroom and a shower room on one floor. A huge roof terrace occupied the floor immediately above – a space that was rarely used because of poor access.

Existing problems

- the **entrance lobby** did not comply with Fire Regulations and was therefore illegal

- the **kitchen** had recently been refitted to a very high standard and, although small, it was not to be touched for budget reasons

- the **living room** was spacious but felt slightly dark because of the location of the windows at the corners of the room. The fireplace was in an awkward position for furniture layout

- the **master bedroom** was small and uninteresting

- the **guest bedroom** was small and badly laid out, with the built-in closet poorly positioned in terms of aesthetics and location

- the **bathrooms** had to be kept within the same general area to avoid the cost of moving services

- the **roof terrace** was accessible only via awkward, steep steps up, making it difficult to use on a regular basis

ORIGINAL FLOOR PLAN

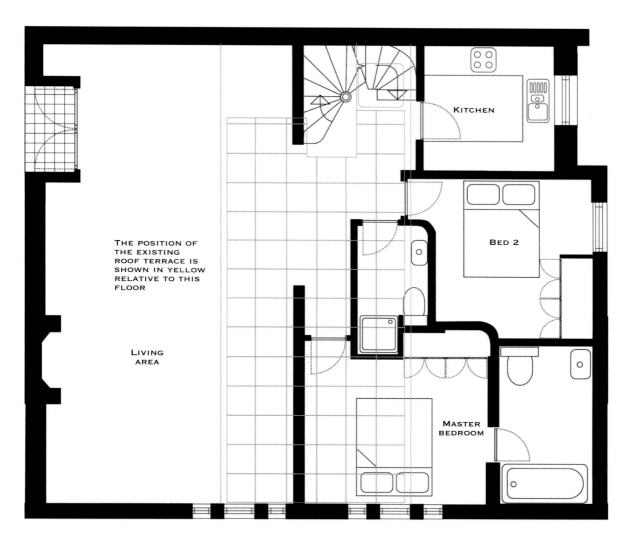

THE POSITION OF THE EXISTING ROOF TERRACE IS SHOWN IN YELLOW RELATIVE TO THIS FLOOR

LIVING AREA

KITCHEN

BED 2

MASTER BEDROOM

Objectives

- to give the existing apartment a modern, spacious feel to complement the views

- to create maximum entertaining space, while still accommodating a constant stream of visitors

- to increase the number of bedrooms from two to four without compromising open-plan objective

- to convert part of the roof terrace into habitable space, but still maintain a small outdoor space

- to ensure that there would not be any negative impact on the apartment's market value as creating too many bedrooms within a given space can affect a property's saleability

Sliding a two-bedroom apartment into four with large entertaining space

A flexible space was created – with movable partitions – to give the owner two contrasting solutions to meet his requirements to have both maximum entertainment space, and accommodate his many regular visitors. When the property was in entertaining mode, the partitions would be open, allowing maximum circulation space. When accommodation mode was the order of the day, the partitions could be closed, creating separate bedrooms, as required.

ENTERTAINING MODE REVEALS:

▌ the **entrance lobby** now conforms to Fire Regulations

▌ the **kitchen** is unchanged

▌ the **reception room** presents as a panoramic room with:
  – a **study/home cinema** area to the far right of the reception door, and
  – **additional entertaining space** to the far left, with built-in sofa and a
  – **second bathroom**

▌ the only hints that any of this large reception area transforms into two further bedrooms are discreet floor-to-ceiling **acoustic panels** to the right of the reception room door, and a floor-to-ceiling sandblasted **glass partition panel** to the left of the reception door

▌ the **master bedroom** and **en-suite bathroom** with a floor-to-ceiling built-in closet. The base of the closet serves as storage space for half of the pull-out double bed base for bedroom 3

ORIGINAL FLOOR PLAN

KEY

▮	BATHROOM
▮	EN-SUITE
▮	MASTER BEDROOM
▮	OTHER BEDROOMS
▮	HALLWAY
▮	KITCHEN
▮	LIVING AREA
▮	STORAGE
▮	STUDY AREA

SECTIONS SHOWING ADDED SKYLIGHT

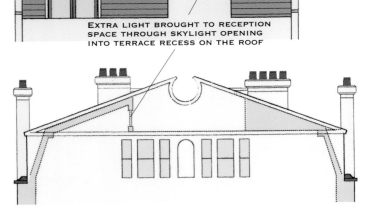

EXTRA LIGHT BROUGHT TO RECEPTION SPACE THROUGH SKYLIGHT OPENING INTO TERRACE RECESS ON THE ROOF

**ENTERTAINING
MODE**

ACOUSTIC
PANELS FOLDED
INTO DOORWAY

SUPPORT FOR
STRUCTURAL BEAM
IN PLACE OF
REMOVED WALL

GLASS
PARTITION IN
OPEN POSITION

BOTTOM OF BED
SERVES AS SOFA
IN ENTERTAINING
MODE

0   5M

Drawing the walls to create the bedrooms

When entertaining has run its course and the numerous guests need to be accommodated in the apartment, full accommodation mode is the order of the day.

Bedroom two is created instantly by folding across the floor-to-ceiling acoustic panels and is then accessed from the entrance lobby. This room can also be created when either a private study or separate home cinema viewing area are required in isolation from the main reception area.
A very comfortable sofa bed serves both the accommodation mode and the entertainment mode by moving its position.

A panel opens for the workstation to slide into the left-hand storage unit. The sofa bed then neatly fits into the empty alcove left by the workstation. The latter is still accessible when the space becomes a bedroom as doors in the unit open to reveal the workstation.

A Zen-style sandblasted glass panel that normally appears as an art piece on the wall opposite the fireplace slides across to form bedroom 3, which includes its own bathroom.

ORIGINAL FLOOR PLAN

KEY

BATHROOM

EN-SUITE

MASTER BEDROOM

OTHER BEDROOMS

HALLWAY

KITCHEN

LIVING AREA

STORAGE

STUDY AREA

ACCOMMODATION MODE

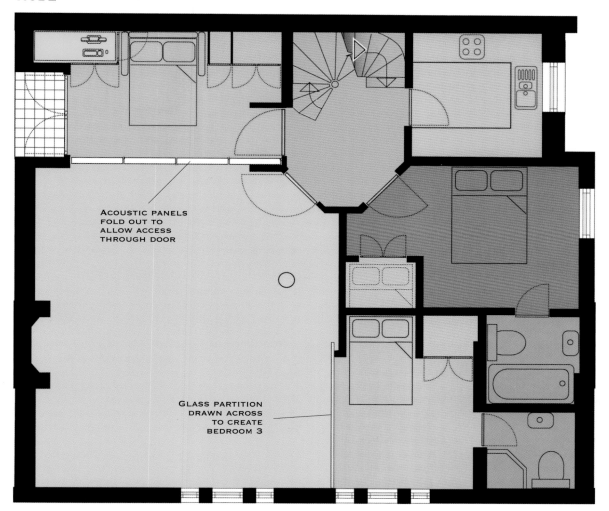

ACOUSTIC PANELS
FOLD OUT TO
ALLOW ACCESS
THROUGH DOOR

GLASS PARTITION
DRAWN ACROSS
TO CREATE
BEDROOM 3

AND IN ACCOMMODATION MODE:

- the **entrance lobby** is unchanged from entertaining mode

- the **kitchen** remains unchanged

- the **reception room** transforms into a smaller reception room with two additional guest bedrooms

- acoustic panels slide across to form **bedroom 2**

- the **workstation** slides into the closet, but is still accessible through its doors

- the sofa bed rotates to occupy this space

- **bedroom 3**, complete with en-suite bathroom, is created by sliding across the sandblasted glass panel

The plan to bring the outside in A roof extension was designed to create a new indoor area that allows maximum light and air flow, while still giving the impression of being outdoors – with the bonus of some retained outdoor space.

ORIGINAL FLOOR PLAN

- **new staircase** in improved position gives easy access to new room above and is wider than the original

- **reception room 2**: the 'entertaining space' and 'accommodation space' brief has also been applied to the roof extension. What appears as a large, light entertaining space with built-in sofa transforms into:

  – **bedroom 4**: as with bedroom 3 downstairs, the built-in sofa in entertaining mode slides out to become a double bed in accommodation mode. The bed head slides into a recess in the eaves when not in use

- repositioning the stairs allowed the inclusion of an **en-suite** shower room, as well as a skylight to light the hallway below

- **small roof terrace**: bi-folding glazed doors can be drawn back, giving access to the area that remains as a roof terrace

- to help create the illusion that the entire area is **outdoor space**, the floor has been tiled throughout in sandstone, with underfloor heating

SIDE ELEVATION

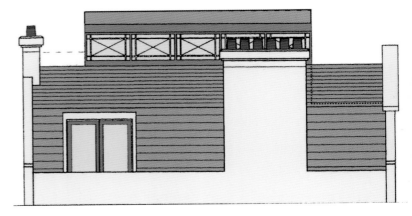

CROSS REFERENCE

SEE ALSO 'VALUABLE SPACE' ON PAGE 36. PLANS WERE ALSO DRAWN UP WITH A VIEW TO PURCHASING THE APARTMENT ON THE FLOOR BELOW AND COMBINING THE TWO PROPERTIES INTO ONE TRIPLEX.

PLAN SHOWING NEW LAYOUT RELATIVE TO FLOOR BELOW

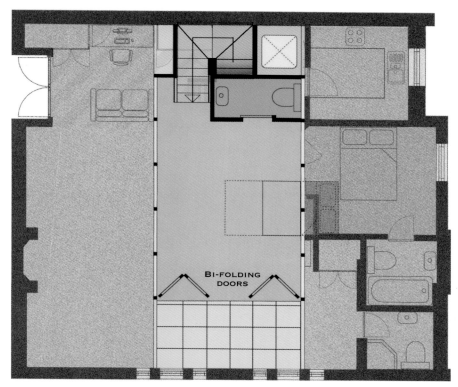

BI-FOLDING DOORS

KEY

	EN-SUITE
	BEDROOM
	HALLWAY
	GLASS

FRONT ELEVATION

0   5M

A top-floor open-plan children's suite

DESIGNERS: PAULA ROBINSON DESIGN GROUP

Accommodating the needs of young children within a family home can cause issues in many houses, particularly as most parents would ideally like to achieve a bedroom for each child and a communal play area. If space allows for the luxury of keeping the play area separate from adult living spaces, there are a number of options that can be achieved by using space as flexibly as possible.

This terraced property offered three children's bedrooms on the top floor of the house with a bathroom on the half-landing leading to the floor below. The layout was not ideal as it made no allowance for any area to play in. Also, accessing a bathroom down a flight of stairs was not safe for young children, especially at night.

Existing problems

■ the three existing **bedrooms** offered no room for a communal playing area for the children

■ the **bathroom** was down a flight of stairs on the half-landing and therefore dangerous for night access by the children

■ **storage space** was lacking

Objectives

■ to create three bedrooms with a separate play area

■ to have a bathroom on the same level as the bedrooms

■ to create maximum closet and storage space

**ORIGINAL
FLOOR PLAN**

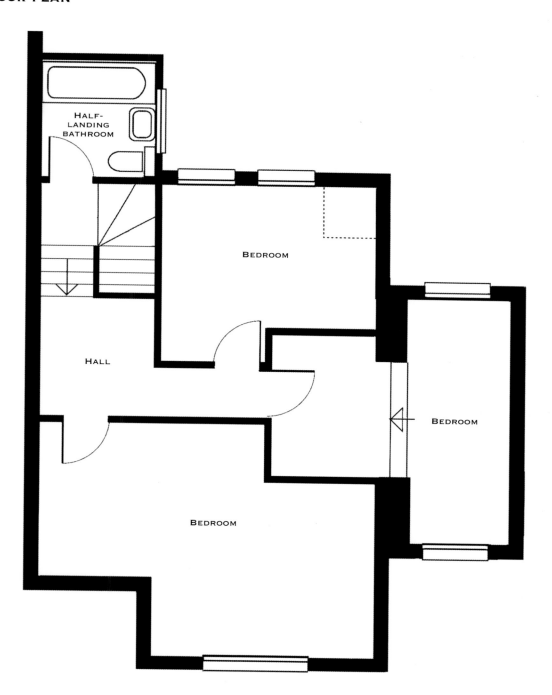

HALF-
LANDING
BATHROOM

BEDROOM

HALL

BEDROOM

BEDROOM

Three bedrooms become an open-plan play area The design solution for this top floor children's suite was to turn the space into flexible space. Only one of the three existing bedrooms was retained because it was sited in the side access extension – and opening this bedroom up would have gained very little space. Instead, most of the walls to the other two bedrooms were removed and replaced by floor-to-ceiling folding doors that, when open, turn the floor into an open-plan space for playing. When closed, they fold across to form acoustic walls to give privacy and definition to two additional bedrooms.

A new bathroom has been created, making use of the doorway that originally served the larger of the three bedrooms. The bathroom does not have a window, but its location on the same floor as the bedrooms compensates for this fact.

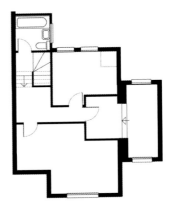

ORIGINAL FLOOR PLAN
KEY

BATHROOM

HALLWAY

CHILDREN'S BEDROOM

STORAGE

- the **landing** is spacious and the bedrooms are a good distance away from the stairs for safety reasons during play time

- the **corridor** is now obvious only when the partitions are closed on the bedrooms. Otherwise, it forms part of the play area, making maximum use of its space

- the reconfigured flexible **bedrooms** alternate between their roles as bedrooms when the floor-to-ceiling acoustic doors are closed, and
  - an open-plan **play area** when the acoustic doors are thrown open and folded against their respective walls. The beds fold away into the walls to disguise all traces of the bedrooms

- the **third bedroom** remains as before, as it is sited in the side extension and could not easily be made part of the open-plan feel of the floor

- the **bathroom** is now on the same floor as the three bedrooms, making it safer for night access. It does not have a window, but its convenient location compensates for this

- maximum **storage space** has been created in all three bedrooms

REVISED FLOOR PLAN

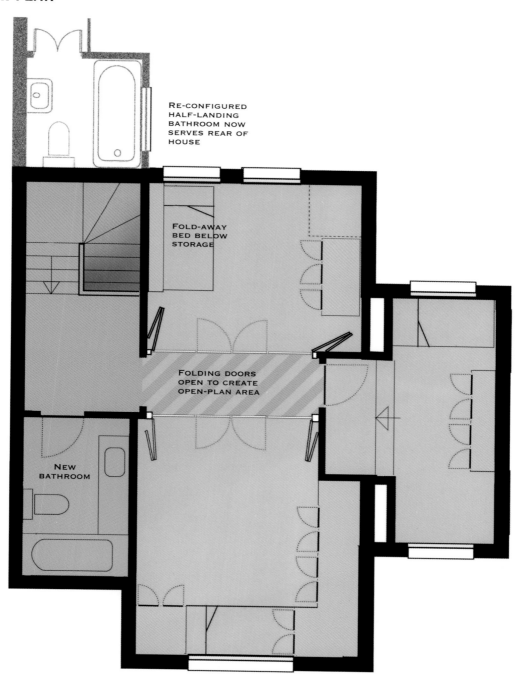

RE-CONFIGURED HALF-LANDING BATHROOM NOW SERVES REAR OF HOUSE

FOLD-AWAY BED BELOW STORAGE

FOLDING DOORS OPEN TO CREATE OPEN-PLAN AREA

NEW BATHROOM

0   5M

...or end up with two larger bedrooms

An alternative to the previous three-bedroom, one-bathroom layout would be to create a two-bedroom, one-bathroom floor plan. This would be an option for a family of only two children, or if the parents preferred to have two of three children sharing one bedroom.

This layout would mean that the bathroom could be located in the side extension, where the former third bedroom was sited. This would obviously be a very bright and airy bathroom with maximum daylight from its four windows. It would also be a much more spacious area, with the additional feature of a built-in baby-changing facility adjacent to the basin. This bathroom does include two steps, which may or may not pose a potential hazard for night-time trips to the bathroom.

- as before, the **landing** is spacious and the two bedrooms are a good distance away from the stairs for safety reasons during play time
- the **corridor** is now obvious only when the partitions are closed on the bedrooms. Otherwise, it forms part of the play area, making maximum use of its space
- the reconfigured flexible **bedrooms** alternate between their roles as bedrooms when the floor-to-ceiling acoustic doors are closed, and
  - an open-plan **play area** when the acoustic doors are thrown open and folded against their respective walls. The beds fold away into the walls to disguise all traces of the bedrooms
- the **bathroom** is now on the same floor as the two bedrooms, in the space previously occupied by the third bedroom. It has a spacious layout and includes a baby-changing facility next to the basin
- maximum **storage space** has been created in both bedrooms

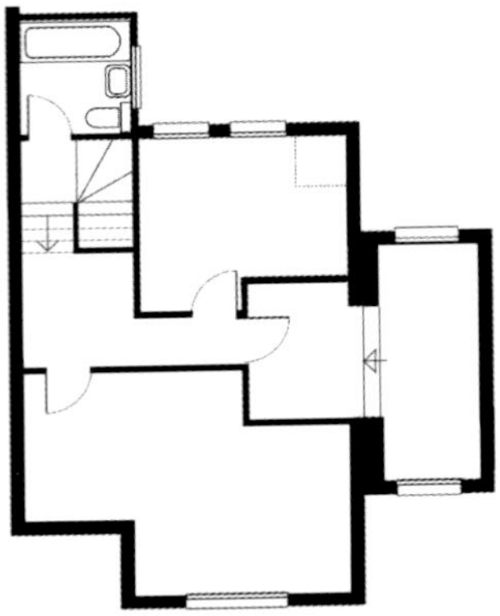

ORIGINAL FLOOR PLAN

KEY

- BATHROOM
- HALLWAY
- CHILDREN'S BEDROOM
- STORAGE

CROSS REFERENCE

SEE ALSO PAGE 162, WHERE USE WAS MADE OF THE HALF-LANDING BATHROOM TO CREATE A SELF-CONTAINED GUEST SUITE IN THIS SAME PROPERTY. THE CHANGES THERE ADDED A ROOM WHICH BALANCED OUT THE LOSS OF A BEDROOM ON THIS FLOOR.

REVISED FLOOR PLAN

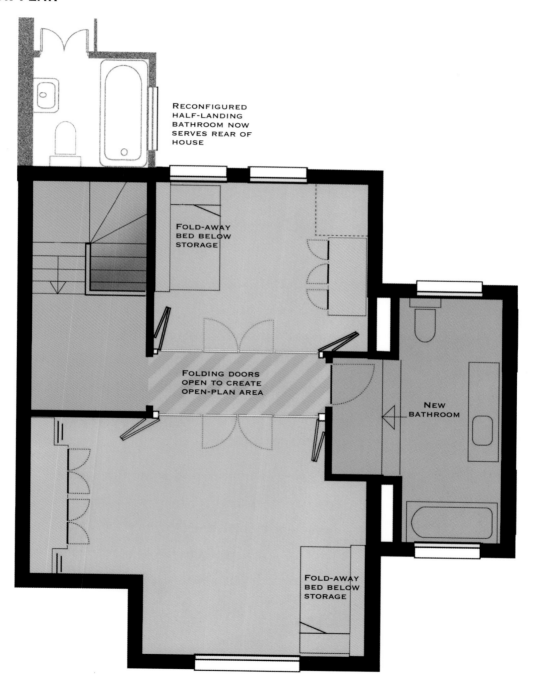

RECONFIGURED HALF-LANDING BATHROOM NOW SERVES REAR OF HOUSE

FOLD-AWAY BED BELOW STORAGE

FOLDING DOORS OPEN TO CREATE OPEN-PLAN AREA

NEW BATHROOM

FOLD-AWAY BED BELOW STORAGE

O   5M

How a few subtle changes can make all the difference

ARCHITECT: JONATHAN CLARK

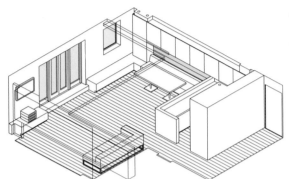

This two-bedroom apartment offered reasonable accommodation but with a few drawbacks. The living/dining area felt compartmentalized despite being open plan, and the position of the small kitchen segregated the living and dining areas without room for flexibility.

A lot of square footage was devoted to the entrance hallway, which was very wasteful of space. Having two equally sized bathrooms was unnecessary given the size of the rest of the apartment. The en-suite bathroom encroached too much on the master bedroom's floor space. The second bedroom was a bonus for guests, but was not put to regular enough use to justify the space used.

The requirement for reconfiguring this apartment was to create flexible space that would give a large, open-plan feel while still being practical. Retaining two bedrooms was essential, but the second bedroom needed to be part of everyday space when not in use by guests.

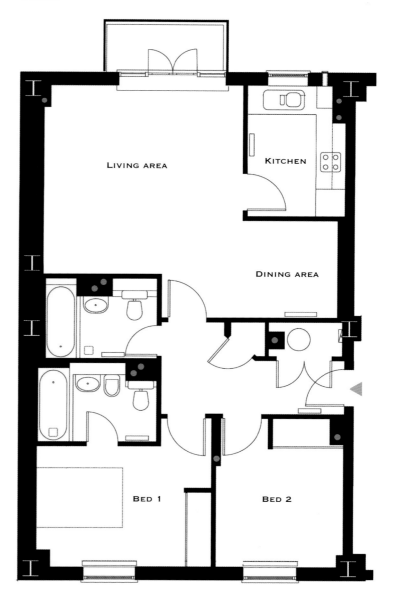

LIVING AREA

KITCHEN

DINING AREA

BED 1

BED 2

Existing problems

▌ the **entrance hall** was wasteful of space

▌ the **living/dining area** was not effective or free-flowing

▌ the **kitchen** was small and divided the living/dining space unnecessarily

▌ it was not necessary for the **bathrooms** to be the same size

▌ the **master bedroom** lost space to the bathroom

▌ **closet** and **storage** space was badly planned

Objectives

▌ to create a large open-plan **living/dining area**

▌ to create flexible space to accommodate guests when required, but without sacrificing space to a guest bedroom on a daily basis

▌ to reduce the size of at least one of the **bathrooms**

▌ to turn the **hallway** into usable space where practicable

A larger master suite

The apartment has been designed to give a contemporary, open-plan living space for a couple. The former living/dining area and separate kitchen have been redesigned to offer a large living area opening out onto the terrace, with a dining area complete with built-in fixed seating beneath overhead storage. This solution minimizes loss of space to dining chairs. The new kitchen occupies space formerly taken up by the dining area and hall closet space. The second bathroom has been reconfigured, has a new sliding door and now offers a double-basin vanity unit. The en-suite bathroom has been reduced in size and converted to a shower room so it no longer encroaches on master-bedroom space.

The master bedroom appears to occupy the entire width of the apartment, with only a single wall panel dividing it from what can be seen as a large dressing area. Both areas are accessed by sliding doors to minimize space loss. All available wall space has been devoted to floor-to-ceiling closets and storage.

ORIGINAL FLOOR PLAN

KEY

BATHROOM

MASTER BEDROOM

HALL

KITCHEN

LIVING AREA

EN-SUITE

STORAGE

UTILITY DUCT

▮ the **hallway** has now been reduced in size. All doors are sliding, except to the main living area

▮ the **living/dining area** is now spacious and practical, with a fixed seating area for dining

▮ the **kitchen** is larger and no longer segregates the living area

▮ **bathroom 2** has been reconfigured to include double basins and has an etched glazed panel to

bring in light from the living area

▮ the **en-suite shower room** replaces the space-wasting en-suite bathroom, and includes an illuminated glazed panel to the hallway

▮ the **master bedroom** appears spacious, with built-in closets and a central division from:

– the **dressing area**, with maximum floor-to-ceiling closet space

**REVISED
ONE-BEDROOM
LAYOUT**

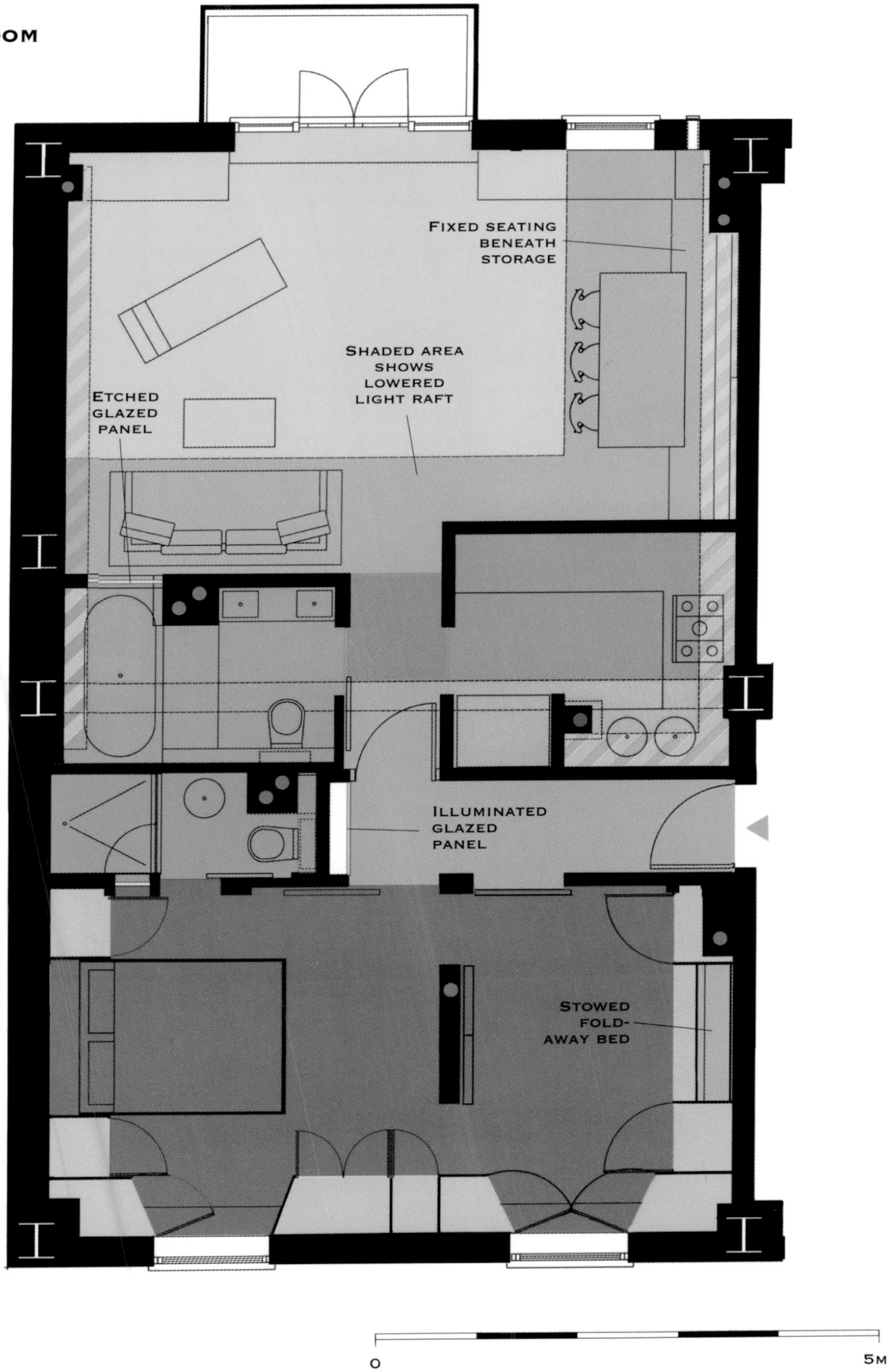

FIXED SEATING
BENEATH
STORAGE

ETCHED
GLAZED
PANEL

SHADED AREA
SHOWS
LOWERED
LIGHT RAFT

ILLUMINATED
GLAZED
PANEL

STOWED
FOLD-
AWAY BED

0   5M

Sliding the guests in

The apartment can be converted quickly and easily into a two-bedroom property by sliding out two partitions from the central division in the master suite. A fold-away bed is pulled down to provide accommodation for guests in the newly formed second bedroom.

This flexible space creation does not detract from the master bedroom, apart from losing its separate dressing area. The sliding doors to all bedrooms and bathrooms ensure that the apartment continues to feel spacious.

The rest of the apartment remains as previously shown.

ORIGINAL DECK PLAN

KEY

	BATHROOM
	BEDROOM
	MASTER BEDROOM
	HALL
	KITCHEN
	LIVING AREA
	EN-SUITE
	STORAGE
	UTILITY DUCT

ISOMETRIC VIEW SHOWING KITCHEN AND LIVING AREA

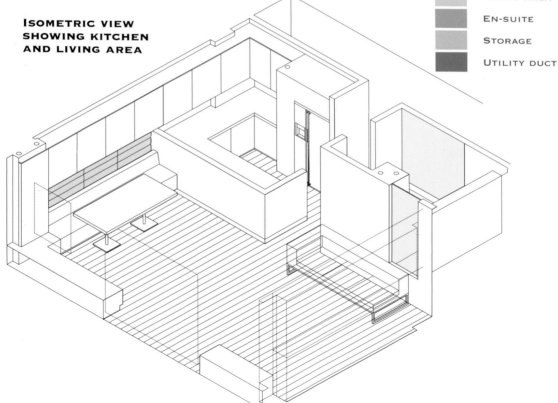

REVISED TWO-BEDROOM LAYOUT

- the entrance, living/dining area, kitchen and bathroom 2 remain as previously configured

- the **master suite** now converts into a master bedroom and shower room separated from:

- **bedroom 2** by sliding partitions, which are pulled out from the floor-to-ceiling central panel in the master suite. A fold-away bed is pulled down to provide accommodation in bedroom 2

- **sliding doors** to the two bedrooms and bathrooms ensure a maximum sense of space and flow

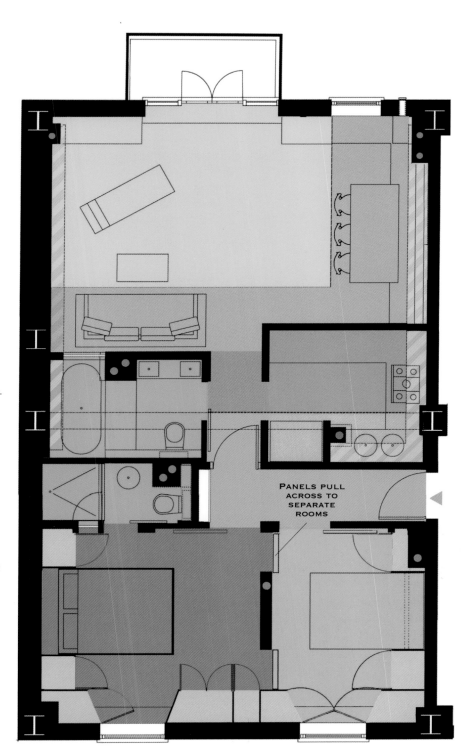

PANELS PULL
ACROSS TO
SEPARATE
ROOMS

0   5M

For seafarers: flexible space working on board a yacht

CONCEPT: PAULA ROBINSON DESIGN GROUP

When a former US President's sleek, beautiful yacht required updating and refitting for new owners, a creative solution was sought for the master cabin. A lot of space was taken up by ablution facilities. These were divided between two separate master 'heads': Jacuzzi bath, basin and toilet in 'hers'; shower, basin and toilet in 'his'.

The yacht was to be chartered when not in use by the new owners. However, as shown by the passenger section of the original deck plan, its configuration only provided accommodation for six people. For maximum income, it needed to sleep up to eight people when in charter mode. A flexible solution was required to ensure no loss of space in the master cabin when the owners were on board.

Existing problems

- the **master cabin** needed to be updated and reconfigured

- the **master heads** (bathrooms) were wasteful of space and divided into 'his' with shower, basin and toilet; 'hers' with Jacuzzi, basin and toilet

- the long **passage** to the master cabin and heads was wasteful of space

Objectives

- to reconfigure the cabins of the yacht to provide flexible accommodation for up to eight people

- to divide the existing space to offer additional berths for charter mode, but to maintain the spacious feel of the master cabin for when the owner would be on board

- to include full facilities: separate bath and shower, maximum closet space, dressing table and seating

ORIGINAL DECK PLAN

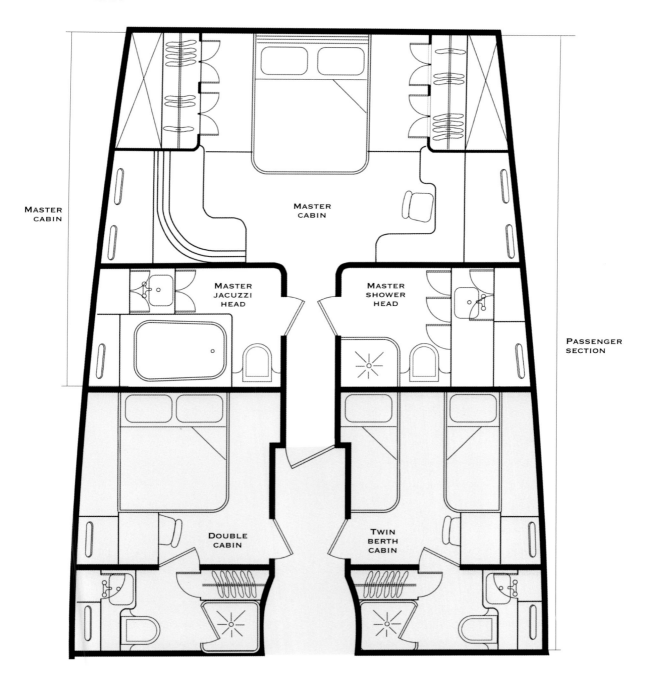

MASTER cabin

MASTER CABIN

MASTER CABIN

MASTER JACUZZI HEAD

MASTER SHOWER HEAD

PASSENGER SECTION

DOUBLE CABIN

TWIN BERTH CABIN

Keeping the owners comfortable

Three factors needed to be taken into account when planning this reconfiguring: symmetry – to help maintain balance along the keel; maximum use of available space (no matter how small); and easy access to, and operation of, any movable equipment to simplify the crew's tasks.

The focus of the solution was confined to the master cabin as nothing could be gained by changing the double and twin berths. It was structurally possible to reposition the two master heads aft, thereby losing the long passage and maximizing the sense of space and light within the master cabin. The solution presents as an open-plan suite with a glazed acoustic panel dividing the large double berth area on one side from the comfortable living area on the other.

An unusual aspect was the orientation of the berth 'athwartships', or across, rather than along the yacht's axis. In smaller vessels this can be uncomfortable if sleeping while under sail. However, the luxury status of this craft meant nights would always be spent at anchor.

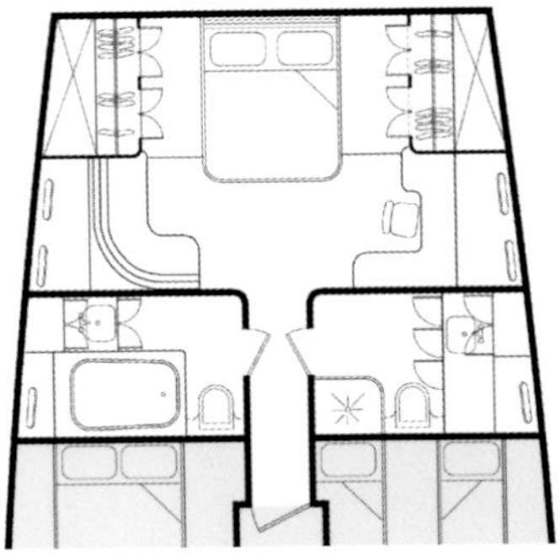

ORIGINAL DECK PLAN

KEY

- MASTER CABIN
- CORRIDOR
- HEAD
- SEATING AREA
- STORAGE
- DESK AREA
- VANITY AREA

- the **entrance** to the master cabin is now double: one door leads to the berth area, the other door to the living area. This makes use of space formerly taken up by a long corridor
- the **berth area** has a fixed queen-size bunk with built-in bedside storage pods and lights. A rise-and-fall television unit, a dressing table and seating are all housed in the unit opposite the berth
- built-in closets flank the entrances to 'his' and 'hers' **heads** with built-in vanity unit and toilet. One facility has a bath, the other a shower
- the **living area** is divided from the berth area by a glazed acoustic panel which also serves as a headboard. The area can be accessed from either side of the berth area. A comfortable sofa backs onto the glazed dividing wall. Facilities on the outer bulkhead echo those on the berth side
- **storage** pods are attached to the side of the glazed panel and can be raised or lowered – and folded in towards the panel – to give more clearance

OPTION 1
OWNER'S CABIN MODE

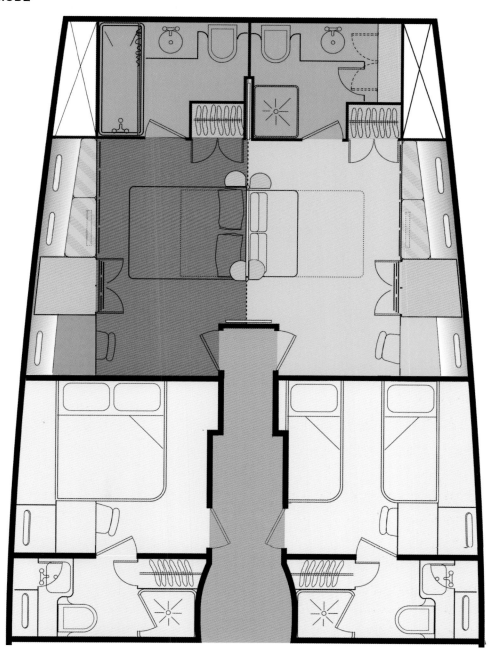

0   5M

Splitting the master suite into two double berths

For the crew, transforming the layout of the yacht to cater for charter mode and an increased occupancy has to be a relatively quick and easy procedure – without the need to store cumbersome additional bulkhead sections on board.

The division of the space into two separate cabins is achieved by 'creating' a fixed wall between the two berths. A recess between the two heads houses one acoustic panel that slides out and locks into place onto the permanent glazed panel division. A second acoustic panel folds out from its position against the entrance bulkhead and locks into place onto the other side of the glazed divider. The former sofa slides outwards to reveal a stowed mattress and converts into another double berth. This locks into position complete with its own bedside pods.

ORIGINAL DECK PLAN

KEY

▦	MASTER CABIN
▦	CHARTER CABIN
▦	CORRIDOR
▦	HEAD
▦	SEATING AREA
▦	STORAGE
▦	DESK AREA
▦	VANITY AREA

- the double **entrance** now leads to two separate double cabins

- double **cabin** 1 has the fixed queen-size berth with built-in bedside units and lights. The unit opposite the berth still houses the rise-and-fall television unit and seating, but the dressing table now has to double as a desk area. Built-in closets flank the entrance to:
  - the **head** with bath, built-in vanity unit and toilet

- double **cabin 2** is divided from cabin 1 by a glazed acoustic panel that folds out from the entrance bulkhead, and a second glazed panel that slides out from between the two heads. Both of these panels lock into position onto the permanent glazed acoustic panel which divides the two areas

- the sofa slides out and converts into a comfortable fixed double berth. The unit opposite berth 2 still echoes that in cabin 1 but now the desk doubles as a vanity area. Built-in closets flank the entrance to:
  - the **head** with shower, built-in vanity unit and toilet

- now that no access is required between the two areas, the side **storage** pods – which can be raised and folded out of the way against the glazed divider – can remain in a convenient position beside the berths

OPTION 2
CHARTER
CABIN MODE

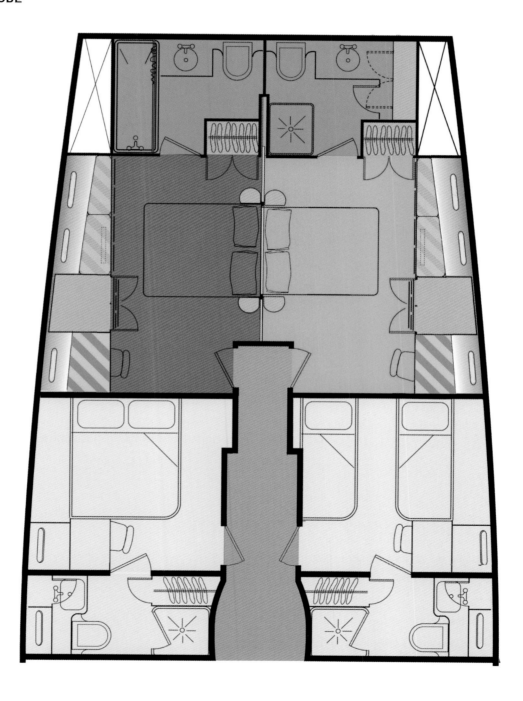

0   5M

Opening up a mini-penthouse

ARCHITECT: JONATHAN CLARK

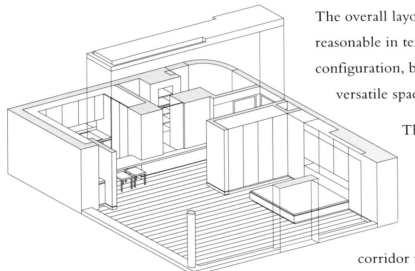

The overall layout of this apartment was reasonable in terms of space and configuration, but a more contemporary, versatile space was required.

The internal corridor, with all rooms leading off it felt dark and restrictive. As the apartment was sited on the top floor, a fire corridor to isolate all rooms from the main entrance was not required.

The bathroom had a predictable, uninteresting layout. The bedroom did not have enough closet space. The kitchen felt awkward if even a small dining table was placed in the area.

The entire apartment needed to be rethought to provide state-of-the-art contemporary living.

Existing problems

▮ the **hallway** was dark and not strictly necessary

▮ the **bathroom** layout was uninteresting

▮ the **bedroom** lacked closet space and the door opened awkwardly onto the bed

▮ the **kitchen** lacked worksurfaces and definition from the living area

Objectives

▮ to create a contemporary one-bedroom home

▮ to create original **bathroom** and **kitchen** layouts

▮ to include central air conditioning in the property

▮ to create maximum closet and storage space

▮ to make the apartment feel open plan, while still considering privacy

ORIGINAL
FLOOR PLAN

KITCHEN/
DINING
AREA

BATHROOM

SERVICE
DUCTS

LIVING
AREA

BEDROOM

Defining the areas with ceiling levels

The key to creating an open-plan feeling – with flexibility – in this one-bedroom apartment was playing with the ceiling levels to give definition to the different areas.

The former entrance to the bedroom was removed – together with the back wall – allowing the bedroom to open directly onto the main living area. When privacy is required, ceiling-mounted screens pull across from the side of the closet wall to shield the bedroom from view.

The living and bedroom areas are defined by two light domes – distinct breaks in the area of lowered ceilings with concealed lighting to demarcate them. The ceiling over the hallway is lowered further and runs into the kitchen/living area. It has a dual purpose: it houses the air conditioning system, which vents into all areas of the apartment, and it also creates an architectural feature. It rests on a standalone pillar, which in turn offers separation between the kitchen and living areas.

ORIGINAL FLOOR PLAN

BATHROOM

BEDROOM

HALL

KITCHEN

LIVING AREA

STORAGE

SERVICES DUCT

- the **entrance** has been opened up and now includes a lowered ceiling that is both an architectural feature and the housing for the air conditioning system

- the **bathroom** has been reconfigured to give a consolidated, contemporary feel that is practical and aesthetically appealing. The bath with shower has two sliding panels on either side of the tub as a novel alternative to the more usual shower screen. The toilet's new position cleverly contributes to the new symmetrical layout of the bathroom

- the entrance to the **bedroom** has been moved to the living area. The bedroom is now open plan and benefits from extensive views to the front and to the side, while still having a privacy option thanks to ceiling-mounted screens that pull across to separate it from the living space. Extensive closet space has been added

- the **kitchen** has been extended but now has more definition thanks to the dining bar and architectural pillar

- the living and sleeping areas are defined by **light domes** – full-height ceiling areas with concealed lighting that wash the spaces with mood light

REVISED
FLOOR PLAN

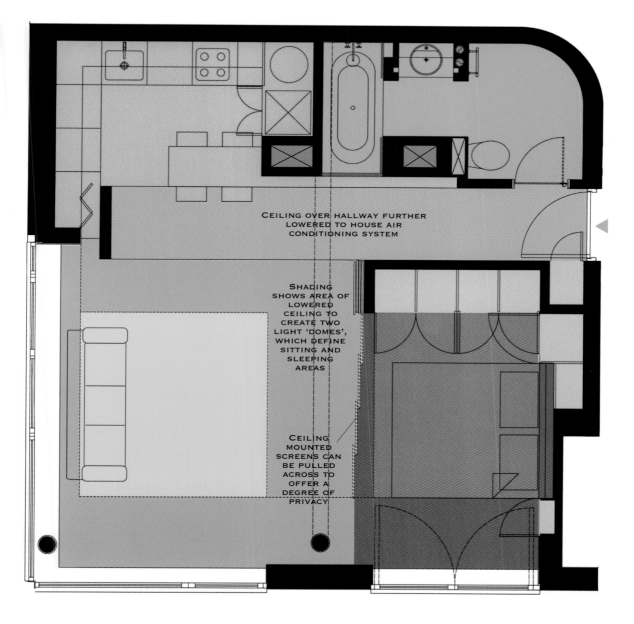

CEILING OVER HALLWAY FURTHER
LOWERED TO HOUSE AIR
CONDITIONING SYSTEM

SHADING
SHOWS AREA OF
LOWERED
CEILING TO
CREATE TWO
LIGHT 'DOMES',
WHICH DEFINE
SITTING AND
SLEEPING
AREAS

CEILING
MOUNTED
SCREENS CAN
BE PULLED
ACROSS TO
OFFER A
DEGREE OF
PRIVACY

0   5M

HIGH-PERFORMANCE SPACE

*Making maximum use
of available space*

Making maximum use of the space that you have available in your home often requires more than a little lateral thinking, and frequent use of the tricks of the trade. With so many people now living alone – but wanting to live in good neighbourhoods in cities where property is exorbitant in price – strategies for maximizing space are essential. Conversions of former large houses into apartments have brought design problems along the lines of how to adapt a former large period reception room into a single flat that includes sitting, sleeping, bathing and cooking areas for one. The dilemmas are endless.

Conversely, families are seeking to adapt large houses to the evolving needs of growing children – without living through several costly and time-consuming reconfigurations. Many choose to transform a house that had previously been converted into flats back into a family home. Achieving this without compromising overall value can be a challenge.

Any space, no matter how small or awkward, can be transformed. But to make a space truly work and perform, we need to address all of its components in isolation. Two of the most important to look at are shape and colour. We take them for granted and never really question them, or the effect that they can have on us and the transformation of our homes. Understanding them can unlock a world of possibilities. And, as technology moves relentlessly forward, they – and their evolution – will become increasingly important.

Looking ahead

The shape of things to come

First, let's consider shape. Convention has instilled in us the preconceived idea that our homes and the rooms within them should be basically either rectangular or square. We have the Greeks and the Romans to thank for this enduring tradition, known as monument architecture, in which façade and appearance were all-important. Monument architecture worked while space was not at a premium and when people's lifestyles were very different.

In our century, limited space – at prohibitive prices per square metre – and dramatically different lifestyles have forced us to re-evaluate the configurations of our homes. Getting the maximum and the best out of the sometimes minimal space available is teaching us to become very creative within these constraints. We are finding that squares and rectangles cramp our style these days. Dividing our homes with the help of curves, circles and any number of angles instead is helping to serve our needs and aspirations in new and exciting ways.

PROBLEM-SOLVING WITH CURVES

Flowing lines and shapes lend a certain flexibility to homes and allow spatial problems to be overcome creatively, rather than traditionally.

Squeezing a bathroom, instead of shower room, into a small one-bedroom flat can be achieved if you are designing with innovative, free-flowing lines rather than perfect right angles. The results can be visually intriguing, and can also increase property value – a flat with a bath is always more saleable than a flat with just a shower, for instance.

THE PSYCHOLOGY OF SHAPES

Stepping away from the straight lines of monument architecture is supposedly good for our mental well being too. Psychologists have gone to great lengths to show that the shapes that surround us are critical to our psychological state. The 'never-ending' line is highly recommended for the internal architecture of homes, especially the kidney shape, favoured for its softness and flexibility.

It has been proved that curves dispel irritability, depression and brain fatigue. Apparently, this is to do with the fact that the human eye responds more quickly to and moves more easily along a curve than a straight line.

CIRCLES: A POWERFUL TOOL

Western architecture has shied away from the circle until now. Ancient and tribal cultures have acknowledged it as the most powerful of shapes, and it has always had deep ritualistic and ceremonial significance.

An American Indian defined it this way:

> Everything the Power of the World does is done in a circle. The sky is round, and I have heard that the earth is round like a ball, and so are all the stars. Our tepees were round like the nests of birds, and these were always set in a circle, the nation's hoop, a nest of many nests, where the Great Spirit meant for us to hatch our children. But the Waischus have put us in these square boxes. Our power is gone and we are dying, for the power is not with us any more.

SHAPING THE WAY FORWARD

Today, we experiment with different kinds of geometry to reach a meeting point in space: the bowed, flowing shape of one wall reaching for the rigid straightness of another wall. Surprise and intrigue keeps the eye and mind alert – there is nothing boring or predictable about shapely lines!

At long last, the rectangle and the square are old news and the circle is being used with less trepidation. Architecture is beginning to achieve a sense of continual flow, with no obvious beginning or end to shapes and structures. As such, the circle is proving easier to live with than the functionalism of the rectangle.

Shape complemented by colour Now let's consider the effects of colour in the home – beyond the obvious 'what's trendy' and what the latest makeover show has recommended. Today, we often think of colour as a simple, straightforward component in a room. It is actually one of the most complex and intangible elements to influence a space.

THE COMPLEXITY OF COLOUR

A colour has many shades – with varying hues, intensities and tones – and it is never exactly the same at any given moment in a day. A turquoise wall will alter dramatically in appearance depending upon the light falling on it; at sunrise, at midday, at dusk, in artificial light, it is a different wall altogether. Perhaps it's the impermanence that lends colour its fascination and appeal.

Colour is highly personal; what attracts one individual will repel another. We often dress our homes as we dress ourselves: exuberant, retiring, adventurous, reticent.

We also follow the dictates of nature: a preponderance of dark colours and hues in cold climates, a riot of bright, sparkling colours and shades in warm climates – a throwback perhaps to animal instinct and the need for camouflage, to blend in with the surrounding landscape?

THE PSYCHOLOGY OF COLOUR

Colour has an amazing ability to alter our mood and perceptions. The psychology of colour is as much a science as it is an art form, with almost as many variations and subtle nuances as there are colour shades and hues.

Research has proved that people are affected by colour not only psychologically, but also physically. It is believed this is

Blue has a sedative, relaxing influence and helps to focus the mind and the intellect. It is known to calm the central nervous system, reducing blood pressure and heart rate, and is excellent for alleviating stress.

Green is acknowledged to have soothing, harmonizing effects. Reminiscent of nature, it is the easiest colour on the human eye and is wonderful for calming all emotional states.

Cream is known to stimulate the right side of the brain, thereby encouraging creative work, but without tiring the mind. It creates a sunny but subdued atmosphere that is nurturing, though not intrusive.

Yellow has an effect akin to that of sunlight: it stimulates, rejuvenates and invigorates. Recognized as alleviating depression and mental tiredness, it acts on the left side of the brain, encouraging logic and non-emotional thinking.

Orange is associated with joy and exuberance. It stimulates the appetite while easing fatigue. Therapists use it to treat depression, stimulate the immune system and reduce the perception of pain.

Indigo and **violet** are associated with the healing of the mind and spirit and are often used in healing spaces to create an aura of calm and retreat.

because colours give off their own electromagnetic field and our bodies are highly sensitive to this. In tests, even subjects who are completely blind react to variations in colour.

THE POWER OF COLOUR

Look at the associations with different colours in the box below and consider how they may be applicable to you and your home.

By contrast, black, white and red elicit bolder, stronger reactions in people. Both Western and – particularly – Eastern history are steeped in these colours and their meanings.

Black heightens emotional response and has a power all of its own. It is often associated with authority and control and has the ability to rivet the onlooker's attention, hence its frequent use in the robes of religious leaders. It can also be seductive – think of the allure of the 'little black dress'; frightening – perhaps due to the fear of being left alone in the dark; and imposing – hence the presence of black furniture in many office interiors of the twentieth century. By definition, black is the absence of colour and, as such, it has the effect of absorbing everything else around it.

White is known for its calming properties and has always been associated with purity, but, like black, it has great power. Since white, by definition, is the presence of all colours, it too can have the effect of absorbing everything else around it.

Red is associated with energy, passion, exuberance and vitality. It is wonderful for stimulating the nervous system and the mind, but can be oppressive. It has many ceremonial and religious connotations in the East and will trigger responses in humans as immediate and direct as waving a red cloth at a bull. Like black and white, it is a very powerful colour and makes statements on many different levels.

BRINGING COLOUR INTO THE HOME

We often forget when introducing colour into our homes that a given colour effect is made up of many elements. The perfect turquoise of tropical seas owes its colour not just to the water itself, but to the white sand beneath, the clear sky above, the angle of the sun, the movement of the tide. All contrive to turn the shallow sea an irresistible and inviting colour. When we paint walls and display fabrics, light is unfortunately the only variable that can alter the appearance of the colour.

The secret of deploying colour in our homes also lies in our growing understanding and appreciation of the diversity and complexity of colour in nature. As our lifestyles separate us increasingly from the natural world, our need to recreate nature's soothing and nurturing qualities will intensify, no matter how much we may deny this need.

COLOURING THE WAY FORWARD

From experience, we have learned that living in static, barren, monotone spaces does not help us to perform at our best or feel vibrant and positive. We know that we require contrast, texture and variety to feel stimulated and alive. Our brains need movement and stimulation to stay alert and responsive. Lassitude can easily creep in – what once seemed an inspired room colour can quickly become incongruous with our mood and lifestyle. This is true even of the safer option of whites and creams. It is perfectly possible to wake up one morning, contemplate the tranquillity of a neutral palette and simply crave the excitement of bright colours.

Advances in technology are gradually making it possible to change colour schemes without the time-consuming inconvenience of redecoration and re-upholstery. Fabrics can change colour and, ultimately, paint will too. Dressing to suit a mood will extend beyond the choice of wardrobe to the choice of room setting. The colour palette of the future will consist of more than just shade, hue, intensity and tone; it will encompass depth, diversity and spontaneity of the very medium that engenders the colours. As such, it will give us a richness, variety and originality not previously experienced in man-made colour.

We are now well accustomed to adjusting light levels to suit mood; soon we will be able to alter colour to lift or calm our spirits. Just as Technicolor made black and white film obsolete in the cinema, our growing colour options in this century will turn static paint and fabric colours into dinosaurs.

Depth and diversity will be the cornerstones of our new colour method. We will build on the human need for movement and change by using materials that conduct light in a variety of ways, thereby creating colours that move and change. Architects and designers are starting to use the principles that govern the way a prism refracts light, and adapting them to our walls and surfaces. Imagine the pleasure of glancing up at a wall that is never quite the same at any given second of the day!

Back to the drawing board

With this understanding of how shape and colour are changing and evolving, and how they can and do affect you, you can begin to identify ways in which to use that knowledge to your advantage in your home. You may be surprised at how this understanding can inspire some subtle but very profound changes.

The first trick is to look at your home as objectively and dispassionately as possible, focusing first on shape, then on colour. Take a lateral view when it comes to shape: look at which straight lines in your home might benefit from being altered.

Curves for storage space and bathrooms

Creating storage space is a good place to start incorporating some new ideas, especially in a long, uninteresting corridor. If you build a straight line of cupboards, you will only be making an already rectangular space appear even more constricted.

If the width of the corridor allows, consider building cupboards along a curved or angled line. You will still get your storage space, but your hallway could end up with an interesting feature that – if designed properly – will add character to the area. Colour will then be able to play its role in accentuating the curve of the wall and drawing the eye away from the length and reduced breadth of the hall.

The bathroom is another area that can benefit greatly from

a curved or angled wall. A shapely wall can create enough room for a bath where previously only a shower would fit within the confines of a straight wall.

Dividing space ingeniously

Shape applies as much to what goes on behind the scenes as it does to what immediately catches the eye. Especially when space is tight, it is very important to consider your property as a whole and not just think of each room/area in isolation. Look at how shapes can be used to divide space more effectively, without being obvious.

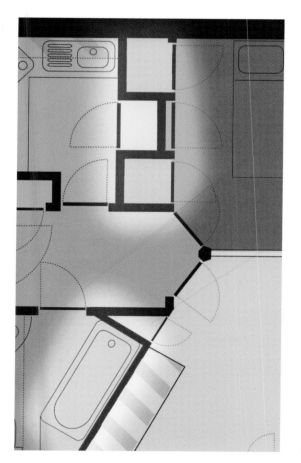

While, at first glance, a row of three floor-to-ceiling wardrobes dividing a bedroom from another room may seem logical and ideal, take a step back and consider how else you might configure your wardrobes. It might make more sense to have only two of the wardrobes accessible for use in the bedroom and to invert the third wardrobe to serve, and be accessible from, the other room.

Moving away from the linear – the accepted classic lines of internal architecture – in both the seen and unseen configuration of your property can have striking aesthetic and practical advantages. Your property will work best if you approach it as a jigsaw puzzle rather than as a square peg to be placed in a square – or even a round – hole.

Annexing side access is Phase I to transforming standard terrace

ARCHITECT: ROSEMONT ARCHITECTURE

This large three-storey end-of-terrace house underwent two major reconfigurations – and two sets of owners – to transform it into the contemporary family home that it now is.

The first owners concentrated on the ground floor and family living area. The current owners took up where they had left off, and set to work on transforming the remaining two floors to match the standard set on the ground floor.

The original house resembled many similar terraced houses except that the rear of the property was much longer than usual.

Existing problems

- the **ground floor** arrangement was very traditional in feel and not practical for a large family looking for contemporary living space

- the **first floor** arrangement was impractical as the two bedrooms had to use the bathroom on the half-landing next to the master bedroom, or the bathroom on the next half-landing up

- the **second floor** arrangement had two bedrooms using the bathroom on the half-landing below

Objectives

- to create additional living space for a large family

- to give the ground floor a more open-plan feel

- to create a separate utility room

- to add at least one other bathroom to serve the first floor

- to take full advantage of the fact that the property was on the end of a terrace and had side access

GROUND FLOOR

FIRST FLOOR

SECOND FLOOR

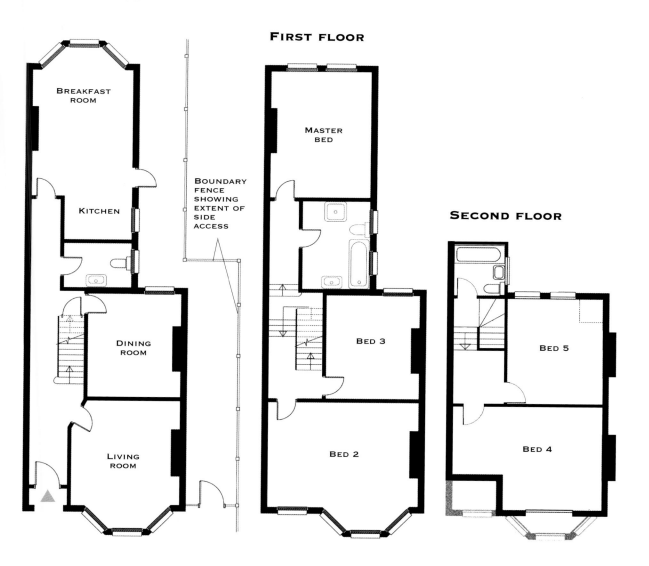

BREAKFAST ROOM

KITCHEN

BOUNDARY FENCE SHOWING EXTENT OF SIDE ACCESS

DINING ROOM

LIVING ROOM

MASTER BED

BED 3

BED 2

BED 5

BED 4

Massive open space created by extensive use of steel beams

Creating contemporary open-plan living space for this house involved the complete removal of the walls of the rear of the ground floor, and the insertion of a rigid steel cage to support the brickwork of the first floor. The dotted lines on the plan show the extent of the reinforcing beneath the walls above.

The original boundary fence to the side access of the property became the outside wall of the newly configured ground floor, adding a side entrance to the house, a utility room and a toilet along the side access passage. In the main area of the new construction, a large open-plan kitchen, dining area and family home cinema area were created, with doors leading out onto the garden. Despite the extension, the garden remained comparatively large.

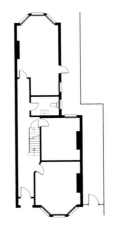

ORIGINAL GROUND FLOOR

KEY

- BATHROOM
- HALLWAY
- KITCHEN
- LIVING AREA
- STORAGE
- UTILITY ROOM

- the **entrance hall** is shorter than before, making it feel more inviting

- the **living room** is the only room on the ground floor that has remained untouched

- the former **dining room** has been incorporated into the open-plan living space as a further seating area around an open fire. It has a cosy feel while remaining part of the open-plan living space

- the new **kitchen** is well laid out and equipped and benefits from light from four skylights running parallel to the new outer wall

- the open-plan **dining area** is large enough to feel formal when necessary, but is very much part of the open-plan living space. The steel support pillars

give a sense of definition rather than separation from the adjoining areas

- the **family area** has an overhead skylight and views onto the garden, and is set around built-in storage, housing audio visual equipment

- the **toilet** is tucked away, but practical for the open-plan living space

- the **utility room** is compact and practical and does not encroach on the open-plan kitchen/ entertaining area

- the **side entrance** is a practical addition to the house, especially for a young family with muddy boots, strollers, etc.

**REVISED GROUND
FLOOR LAYOUT**

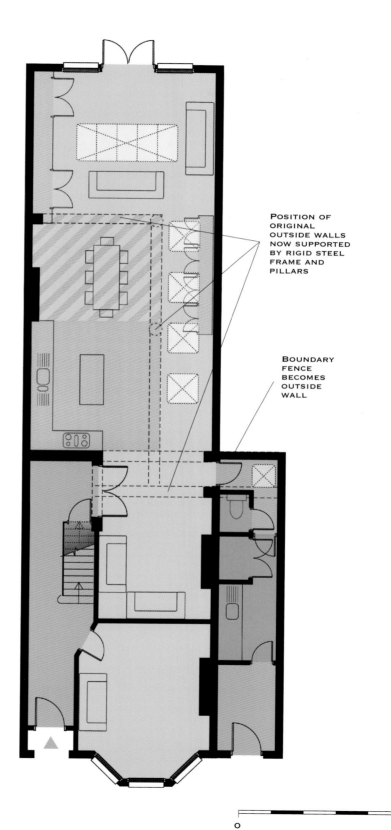

POSITION OF
ORIGINAL
OUTSIDE WALLS
NOW SUPPORTED
BY RIGID STEEL
FRAME AND
PILLARS

BOUNDARY
FENCE
BECOMES
OUTSIDE
WALL

0   5M

Changes bring addition of a bathroom and a study

On the first floor, the new side return extension brought the welcome addition of another bathroom and a small study. This allowed the bathroom on the half-landing between the ground and first floor to become an en-suite facility for the master bedroom – as opposed to a separate bathroom, which formerly served the master bedroom and either of the two bedrooms on the first floor. On the second floor, the side extension added a further bedroom.

Effectively, the house has now gained a bathroom and study or small baby's room, thereby increasing both its value and practicality for a large family with frequent visitors.

ORIGINAL FIRST AND SECOND FLOOR

KEY

	BATHROOM
	EN-SUITE
	MASTER BEDROOM
	OTHER BEDROOMS
	HALLWAY
	STORAGE
	STUDY

- the half-landing between the ground and first floor now houses the **master suite,** with large bedroom and **en-suite bathroom**. The bedroom feels large, because its entrance is now by the half-landing stairs as opposed to beyond the bathroom door as before when this bathroom had to be accessible to the bedrooms of the first floor

- the first floor now has **two bedrooms** as before, although the second bedroom on this floor has become smaller and lost the central location of its fireplace due to:

– the new long **corridor,** which leads to the welcome addition of:

– a further **bathroom** in the new side access extension, and

– a small **study** opposite the bathroom in the side access extension. The study could also serve as a baby's room – it would be too small to classify as a single bedroom

- the second floor has gained a third **bedroom,** bringing the house total to six

REVISED FIRST FLOOR LAYOUT

CROSS REFERENCE

ALSO SEE 'FLEXIBLE SPACE'; PAGES 116-119 FOR ALTERNATIVE LAYOUTS OF THE SECOND FLOOR.

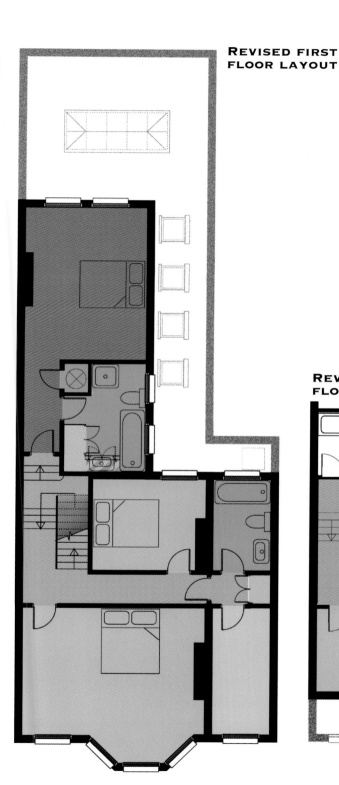

REVISED SECOND FLOOR LAYOUT

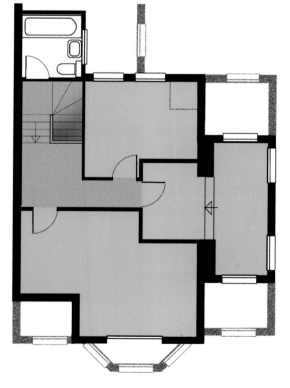

0   5M

An open module option could have worked just as well

Another potential configuration for the master suite and first floor would still have the new side return extension bringing an additional bathroom and small study to the layout. However, it would transform the master suite itself into an open-plan bathing, sleeping and sitting area. This configuration would allow maximum light flow into the suite, with a large bathing area complete with separate toilet for privacy and a wet room. The open-plan feel would help to increase the sense of space and flow within the master suite.

ORIGINAL FIRST FLOOR

KEY

	BATHROOM
	EN-SUITE
	MASTER BEDROOM
	OTHER BEDROOMS
	HALLWAY
	STORAGE
	STUDY

■ the half-landing between the ground and first floor still houses the **master suite**, but with an open-plan design. The bedroom's entrance is still by the half-landing stairs, but

– the en-suite bathroom has become an open-plan **bathing area** complete with a large oval bath tub in the centre of the area, a wet room, a separate toilet, a double-basin vanity unit and closets. Both the separate toilet and the main bathing area have windows. This also floods light into the open-plan corridor leading to:

– the open-plan **sleeping** and **sitting area**. This area has two windows and a fireplace and is spacious enough for a large bed and sofa.

The built-in unit that divides the bathing and sleeping areas has built-in closets on the sleeping side, together with built-in headboard and units above or lighting

■ the first floor has the same configuration of **two bedrooms**, the second bedroom being smaller without its original fireplace due to:

– the new long **corridor,** which leads to the addition of a further **bathroom** in the new side access extension, and

– a small **study** opposite the bathroom in the side access extension. The study could also serve as a baby's room – it would be too small to classify as a single bedroom

OPTIONAL FIRST FLOOR LAYOUT

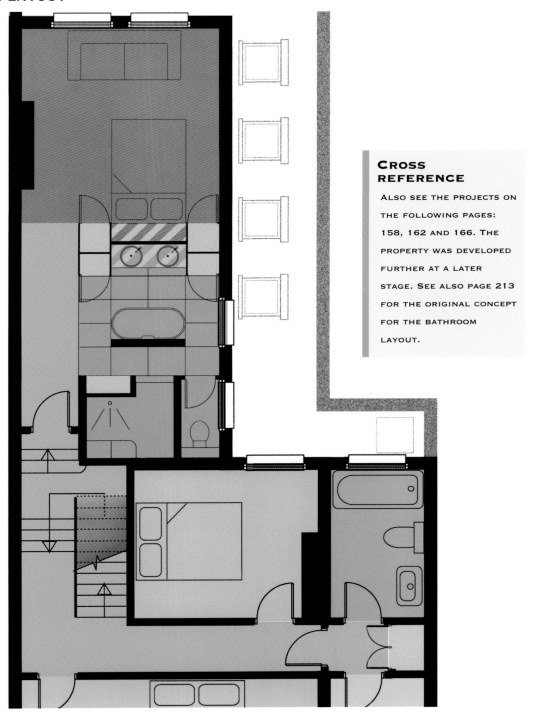

CROSS REFERENCE

ALSO SEE THE PROJECTS ON THE FOLLOWING PAGES: 158, 162 AND 166. THE PROPERTY WAS DEVELOPED FURTHER AT A LATER STAGE. SEE ALSO PAGE 213 FOR THE ORIGINAL CONCEPT FOR THE BATHROOM LAYOUT.

0   5M

Creating a mini-home within the larger house

If the house was to be designed to cater for professional sharers – rather than a young family – a different configuration could be considered for the first floor.

The open-plan bathing, sleeping and sitting areas outlined in the previous pages in the half-landing master suite could also be adapted to the first floor. This would give a very large suite with generous bedroom/living area in the former front bedroom; a large open bathroom with separate shower room and toilet cubicles sited where the smaller bedroom was; and two further areas occupying the former bathroom and study. Sliding glass screens could offer a degree of separation to all these areas but still maintain the open feeling of the suite.

The issue to keep a close eye on with the reconfiguration of the rest of the property would be resale value, as this configuration effectively loses one bedroom – which would need to be made up for elsewhere.

ORIGINAL FIRST FLOOR

KEY

- EN-SUITE
- MASTER BEDROOM
- HALL/ACCESS WAY
- STORAGE
- DRESSING AREA/STORAGE
- GYM/HOME OFFICE

- the half-landing between the ground and first floor still houses a **suite** with open-plan bathing, sleeping and sitting areas

- the **master suite** would, however, be located on the first floor

- a new angled **entrance** gives a more open, inviting feeling to the suite

- the former large bedroom remains the **sleeping** and **sitting** area of the suite, with a storage module placed to offer structural support where the former bedroom/corridor wall has been removed

- this also serves as a visual division between the sleeping area and
  - the **bathing area**, which occupies the former small bedroom and includes a central bath, double-basin vanity unit, separate wet area and separate toilet

- the two further areas are semi-separated by sliding glass screens and could house a **gym**, **dressing area**, **home office**, **storage area** or whatever best suited the individual's needs

OPTIONAL FIRST
FLOOR LAYOUT

0   5M

Phase II - the master suite

DESIGNERS: PAULA ROBINSON DESIGN GROUP

When the next owners of this three-storey end-of-terrace
house moved in, they were faced with a first- and second-
floor configuration that was far from practical for their
contemporary style and needs. The first floor consisted
of a large bedroom with bay windows giving excellent light,
a small guest bedroom with no cupboard, a shoe-box of a
study and a rather cramped bathroom – not to mention
a narrow, dark corridor linking the rooms, complete with
airing cupboard.

The owners very much liked the newly configured open-plan
ground floor as it suited their lifestyle perfectly. Their aim
was to transform the rest of the house to meet the high
standards already set on the ground floor.

CROSS REFERENCE
SEE ALSO PAGE 148 FOR THE
FIRST PHASE OF THIS
TRANSFORMATION

Existing problems

▌ **the corridor** was too narrow and dark

▌ **bedroom 2** was felt to be too large and well
appointed to be used as a guest bedroom

▌ **bedroom 3** was a more appropriate size for a
guest bedroom but the location was not ideal for
the new owners

▌ the **study** was too cramped and tucked away from

the rest of the house for easy daily use. It needed
to be made accessible

▌ the **bathroom** was not well appointed for any of
the rooms on the floor. As a result it was a waste
of prime usable space

▌ the **configuration** of the entire floor felt off-
balance to the new owners and needed to be
completely reassessed

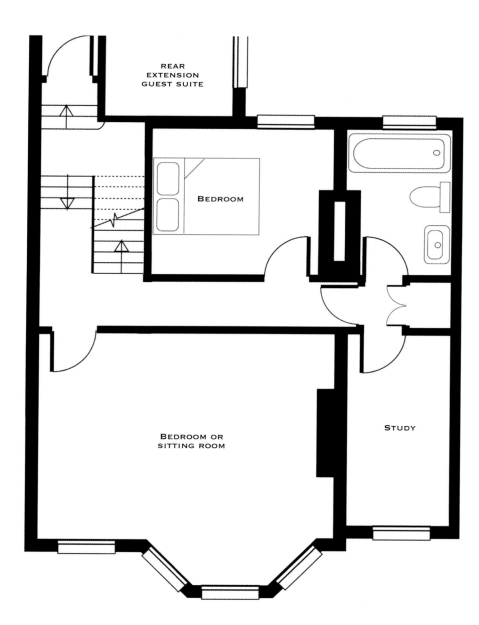

ORIGINAL FIRST FLOOR PLAN

REAR EXTENSION GUEST SUITE

BEDROOM

BEDROOM OR SITTING ROOM

STUDY

Objectives

■ to accommodate the needs of a growing family and achieve a modern, open-plan, airy feel in keeping with the open-plan ground floor

■ to create separate wings throughout the three-storey property – the master suite, the guest suite and the children's suite – each to be self-contained and as versatile as possible

■ to transform the existing first-floor configuration into the master suite

■ to include in the master suite a large bedroom, a dressing area, a large bathroom with separate shower and bath, a study and as much storage space as possible

Creating the master suite

The design of the master suite was inspired by the classic French configuration of a short, wide corridor/lobby lined on both sides with floor-to-ceiling closets, off which all rooms then lead. Space limitations meant that this master suite could not have the typical French-size entrance lobby but, nonetheless, a dressing area was created without encroaching too much on space needed for the suite's other rooms. Each room within the suite was accessed through elegant floor-to-ceiling double doors, used as a space-saving device and also for aesthetic appeal.

ORIGINAL FLOOR PLAN

KEY

▨	BATHROOM
▨	BEDROOM
▨	HALLWAY
▨	STORAGE
▨	STUDY

- the **corridor** doubles as a dressing area, with floor-to-ceiling oak closets on either side. The closets are also excellent for sound insulation between rooms and serve a very practical, technical purpose: as structural support along the line of the bedroom wall for supporting the floor joists above

- the **master bedroom** is an elegant room that makes maximum use of bay window light. Additional storage was achieved by turning all available wall space into concealed floor-to-ceiling closets

- the **study** is now large, airy and easily accessible from the rest of the house. It also doubles as a gentleman's dressing room, with a closet opening into the study instead of the corridor/dressing area

- the **bathroom** features two distinct areas:
  - to the right of the entrance: the open-plan shower (or wet area) and bath
  - to the left of the entrance: double basins and toilet

- **underfloor heating** has been installed

- the suite is **self-contained** and private while still maintaining a flowing, open feeling for its occupants

CROSS REFERENCE
SEE ALSO PAGE 162.
THE CREATION OF A SELF-CONTAINED GUEST SUITE ADDED A BEDROOM, MAINTAINING THE HOUSE'S ORIGINAL FIVE BEDROOMS.

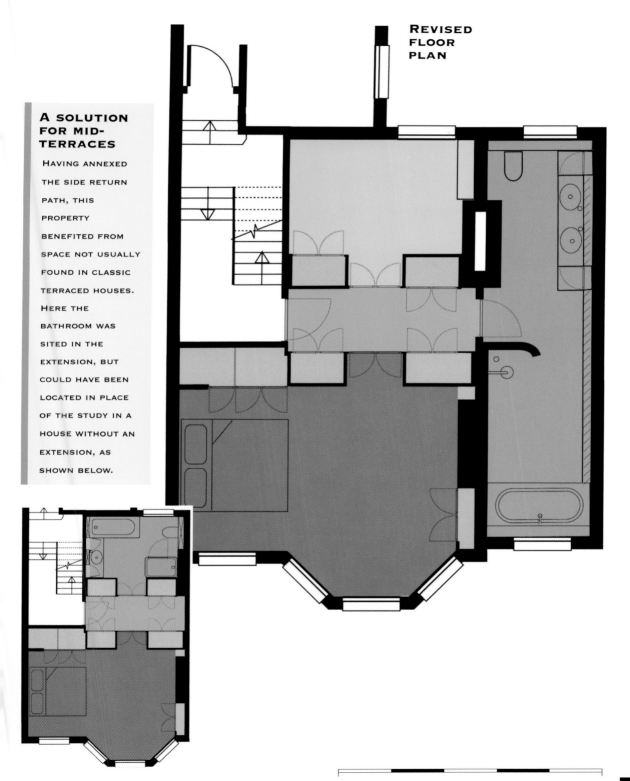

REVISED
FLOOR
PLAN

A SOLUTION FOR MID-TERRACES

HAVING ANNEXED THE SIDE RETURN PATH, THIS PROPERTY BENEFITED FROM SPACE NOT USUALLY FOUND IN CLASSIC TERRACED HOUSES. HERE THE BATHROOM WAS SITED IN THE EXTENSION, BUT COULD HAVE BEEN LOCATED IN PLACE OF THE STUDY IN A HOUSE WITHOUT AN EXTENSION, AS SHOWN BELOW.

0   5M

Phase II - the guest suite

DESIGNERS: PAULA ROBINSON DESIGN GROUP

It was decided that the former master suite on the half-landing between the ground and first floors should be transformed into the guest suite for the house. This new suite needed to include two bedrooms and one bathroom and be separate from the rest of the house.

The existing layout included a long corridor, a large bathroom and a large bedroom. Dividing the space up into two bedrooms and a bathroom would have been too cramped. However, the new plans for the children's suite on the top floor meant that the bathroom on the half-landing between the first and second floors was about to become a 'spare'. Incorporating this spare bathroom into the design of the new guest suite became essential.

Existing problems

- what would become a space-wasting **entrance corridor** leading to the bathrooms beyond the existing bathroom unless reconfigured

- a large **bathroom** with bath and shower which did not leave enough space for two bedrooms unless reconfigured

- a further bathroom on the half-landing above the entrance corridor was redundant within the planned new layout

Objectives

- to create a new guest suite with two bedrooms and one shared bathroom

- to ensure that both guest bedrooms are in proportion with the rest of the property and to minimize loss of everyday usable space

- to make use of the space taken up by the redundant bathroom

- to give the new guest suite a contemporary and interesting feel while still offering a sense of privacy

ORIGINAL FLOOR PLANS

FIRST FLOOR

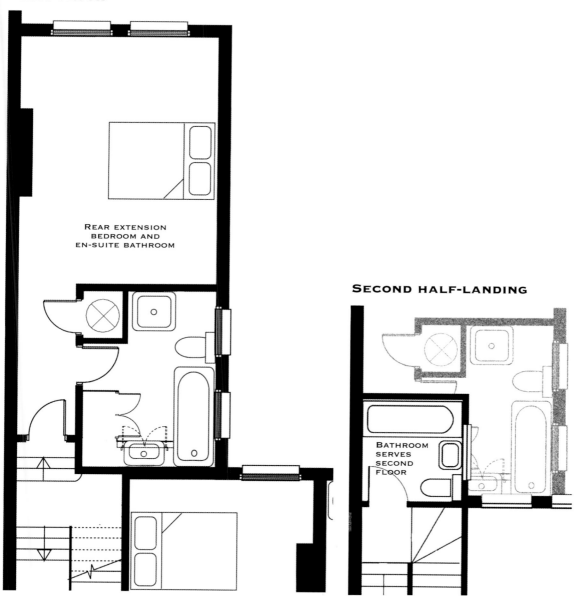

REAR EXTENSION
BEDROOM AND
EN-SUITE BATHROOM

SECOND HALF-LANDING

BATHROOM
SERVES
SECOND
FLOOR

New access route to half-landing bathroom was key to the plan

The owners' requirement for two guest bedrooms sited together with use of one common bathroom went hand in hand with the need to make these rooms as space-efficient as possible. The guest suite was only going to be used occasionally, and therefore sacrificing space to this area was undesirable. However, private guest accommodation separate from the rest of the household was essential.

Once the new master suite was created on the first floor, the old master suite became the ideal candidate for transformation into the new guest suite. However, the existing footprint of the old master suite was too small to comfortably accommodate two bedrooms and a bathroom – despite the brief to minimize space allocated to the guest accommodation.

The new guest suite was created on two levels. The former master bedroom and master bathroom were reconfigured into two guest bedrooms. The redundant second floor landing bathroom was then reconfigured and incorporated into the new suite. This was made possible by means of a staircase leading from the guest floor to the new bathroom. This staircase necessitated additional works in the form of an adjustment to the roof line itself – an expense that was worthwhile given the extent of the works being carried out throughout the rest of the house.

ORIGINAL FLOOR PLANS
KEY

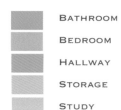

	BATHROOM
	BEDROOM
	HALLWAY
	STORAGE
	STUDY

REVISED FLOOR PLANS

- the **entrance corridor** leads to bedroom 2 and bedroom 3 and the guest bathroom via a staircase

- **bedroom 2** is now a comfortable double guest bedroom with built-in closets sited partly where the original master bedroom was located

- **bedroom 3** is located where the original master bathroom was sited. It makes ideal accommodation for children as either a single bedroom, or a double bedroom with bunk beds. This bedroom now also has built-in closets

- the **bathroom,** although small, is an adequate size for a guest bathroom. Although accessing a bathroom via a staircase can be a problem, it is perfectly acceptable for a bathroom that is not in constant use

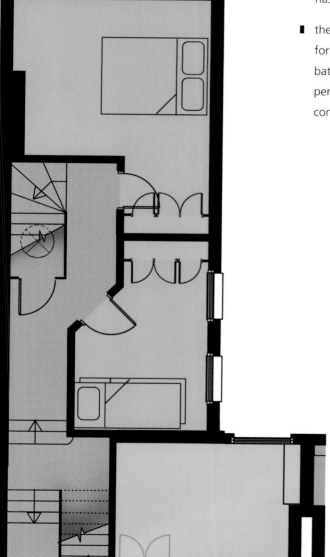

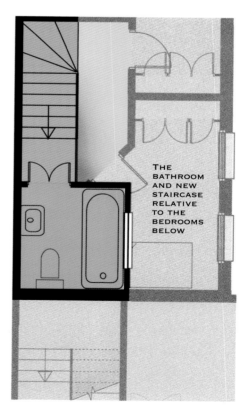

THE BATHROOM AND NEW STAIRCASE RELATIVE TO THE BEDROOMS BELOW

O   5M

Phase II – the children's suite

DESIGNERS: PAULA ROBINSON DESIGN GROUP

The house was configured with three children's rooms on the second floor and a children's bathroom on the half-landing between the first and second floors. The number of rooms coincided nicely with the new owners' intended family size, but the layout of the top floor concerned them and left the huge dilemma of where the children were going to play. The large garden and the family room on the ground floor were a solution, but not always the ideal one.

The clients wanted their children to have an area that was their little world and that did not have to slot into the needs of adult life. This said, they still wanted each child to have their own bedroom. Flexibility was the only possible means of making maximum use of the available space.

Existing problems

- the **landing** and **corridor** were wasteful of space

- the top floor offered **three children's bedrooms** but their configurations could be improved

- the **bathroom** on the half-landing was not ideally located for young children because of the stairs

- there was a lack of **closet** and **storage** space

- there was no area for the children to play

Objectives

- to create three bedrooms and a playing area

- to relocate the bathroom so as to be practical for young children

- to make maximum use of the available space

- to minimize the corridor space

- to create storage and closet space

ORIGINAL
FLOOR PLAN

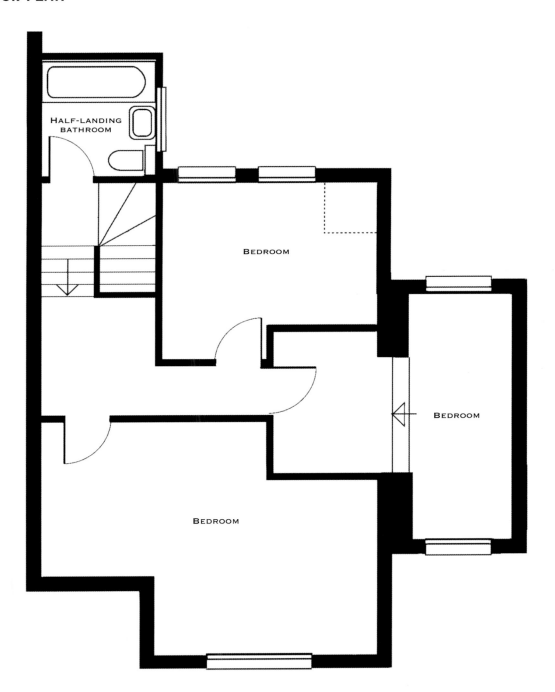

HALF-LANDING
BATHROOM

BEDROOM

BEDROOM

BEDROOM

The children's suite

The design solution for this property involved the use of full-height folding doors, which, when open, turn this top floor into one large open-plan playing area.

When privacy is required, the doors can be pulled closed, thus creating two further separate bedrooms – in addition to the fixed third bedroom. By day, the children have a sense of space and freedom. By contrast, a feeling of cosy safety is reinstated at night with the closing of the folding partitions for sleep time.

- the space-wasting **corridor** has been incorporated into useful space

- floor-to-ceiling folding doors allow the top floor to be transformed from **open-plan play area** by day to:
  - **two further bedrooms** by night, or whenever privacy is required. The folding doors lock into position as walls, complete with double entrance doors to each of the two bedrooms

- the new **bathroom** is now in a practical location on the same floor instead of on the half-landing

- the single bed has been designed to fold away if required, to make the area feel like a playroom by day

- closet and storage space has been created

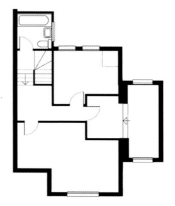

ORIGINAL FLOOR PLAN

KEY

▨	BATHROOM
▨	HALLWAY
▨	CHILDREN'S BEDROOM
▨	STORAGE

CROSS REFERENCE

ALSO SEE 'FLEXIBLE SPACE', PAGE 118; FOR AN ALTERNATIVE LAYOUT TO THIS FLOOR.

REVISED FLOOR PLAN

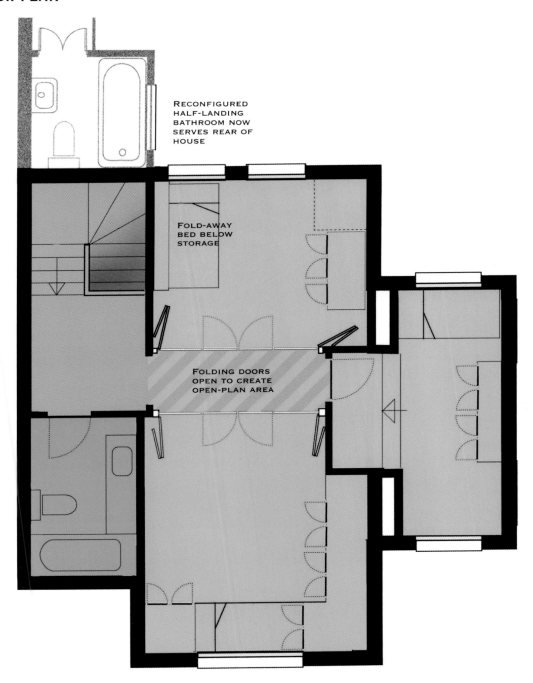

RECONFIGURED HALF-LANDING BATHROOM NOW SERVES REAR OF HOUSE

FOLD-AWAY BED BELOW STORAGE

FOLDING DOORS OPEN TO CREATE OPEN-PLAN AREA

0   5M

Converting a bedroom into two bathrooms for house sharers

ARCHITECT: UV ARCHITECTS

Having an en-suite bathroom for a master bedroom is important both for practical reasons and for resale value. The need becomes even greater when professionals share ownership of their first home – or take in room mates to help share the costs of ownership – and all parties require their own bathroom.

This house presented the classic dilemma of three bedrooms all having to share one bathroom. Worse still, the bathroom was on a half-landing below the bedrooms. The need for two bathrooms in the property could not be got away from, and the budget and property configuration left little scope for any extension work on the lower floors.

Existing problems

- the **two existing bedrooms** sited on the top floor shared one bathroom between them

- the **bathroom** was located on the half-landing below the bedrooms, making it awkward for both bedrooms' use

- the location of the bathroom on the **half-landing** was not only impractical, but also felt dated

- neither bedroom was large enough to incorporate a bathroom or shower room within its footprint

- the conversion of the **loft** into a **third bedroom** added to the need for a further bathroom

- there was no scope for a further facility in the loft conversion, and the available budget made developing the **lower floors** impractical

**ORIGINAL
TOP FLOOR
AND HALF-
LANDING**

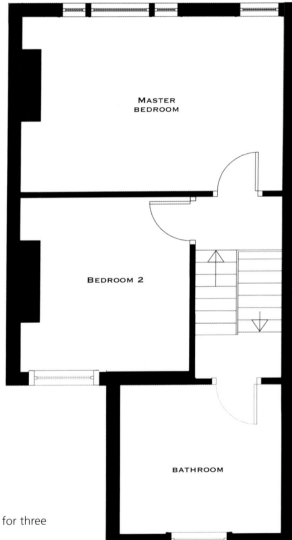

MASTER
BEDROOM

BEDROOM 2

BATHROOM

Objectives

▌ to create two separate bathrooms for three
bedrooms

▌ to ensure that at least one of the bathrooms
would be en-suite

▌ to create a contemporary feel to both the new
bathrooms and the bedrooms

▌ to avoid any compromise of the property's value

Swapping places with the bedroom

The design solution for this property took the unusual step of transforming the second bedroom into two separate rooms: a bathroom accessed from the hallway and an en-suite shower room to the master bedroom. The former bathroom then became the second bedroom.

Dividing a bedroom into two bathrooms can present issues of both light and configuration. In this case, the former bedroom only had one window, so only the new bathroom was able to have a window while the en-suite shower room was without natural daylight. As to shape of the two new rooms, an equal division was impossible because of the position of the staircase in relation to the doorway, and the position of the window. However, maximum use was made of available space by creating alcoves and recesses for towels and toiletries and even stealing space from the master bedroom cupboards to create a vanity cabinet for the shower room.

ORIGINAL FLOOR PLAN
KEY

BATHROOM

EN-SUITE

BEDROOM

HALLWAY

STORAGE

SERVICES

- the second bedroom was turned into an **en-suite shower room** for the master suite and a **separate bathroom** for use by the other two bedrooms

- the former bathroom was turned into **bedroom 2**

- the main bathroom has an unusual configuration because of the division of the space, but includes a well positioned double-ended bath and an unusual corner basin

- while the shower room receives no daylight, the bath benefits from the former bedroom's window

- the en-suite shower room is compact but has all the essentials and borrows storage space from the side of the bedroom cupboard

- the option of a **sliding door** to the en-suite shower room could also be considered to maximize the sense of space

- **bedroom 2** is very compact but is still acceptable in size. Narrow double doors – occupying the original doorway – or sliding doors could be a space-saving device to consider

REVISED
FLOOR PLAN

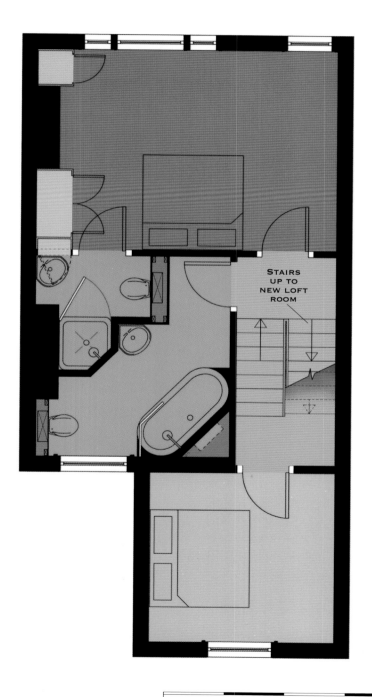

STAIRS
UP TO
NEW LOFT
ROOM

O   5M

From three apartments to six-bedroom luxury home

ARCHITECT: SPENCE HARRIS HOGAN

A large house on four levels had been converted into three apartments. All of the apartments were typical examples of poorly planned conversions: built to maximize the number of rooms, at minimal cost, with no regard for living practicalities.

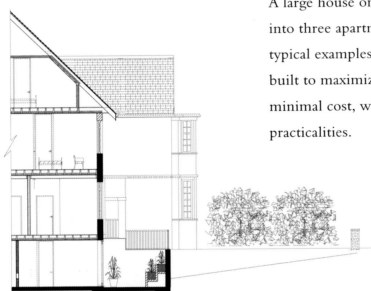

The new owners wanted to transform the property back into one homogeneous house with six bedrooms and five bathrooms, instead of three badly planned apartments.

Existing problems

▌ all **bathrooms** in each of the apartments were ridiculously small – with the exception of the bathroom on the second floor of the duplex which was disproportional to the rest of the rooms

▌ **separate toilets** are an old-fashioned design, impractical and a waste of valuable floor space. For a contemporary property, the toilet should form part of the bathroom itself

▌ the **earth fill** on the lower ground floor was a waste of valuable space

▌ the **garage** only had a narrow access

Objectives

▌ to combine the three separate apartments into one luxury six-bedroom, five-bathroom home

▌ to create a home with four distinct areas: an informal living floor, a formal living floor, a family sleeping floor, and a guest sleeping floor

▌ to redesign the space-wasting rear extension which housed utilities and storage

▌ to address the issue of the earth fill

▌ to widen the garage access to provide off-street parking for two cars

LOWER GROUND APARTMENT

STORAGE AND UTILITY

KITCHEN

LIVING AND SLEEPING AREA

BATH

TOILET

EARTH FILL

GARAGE

GROUND FLOOR APARTMENT

STORAGE AND UTILITY

KITCHEN

LIVING AREA

BATH

TOILET

BED 2

MASTER BED

FIRST FLOOR OF UPPER APARTMENT

TERRACE

KITCHEN

LIVING AREA

BATH

TOILET

BED 2

EN-SUITE

MASTER BED

SECOND FLOOR OF UPPER APARTMENT

BED 3

UTILITY

BED 4

BATHROOM

LOFT STORAGE

The lower ground apartment is turned into informal family living space The lower ground floor has been transformed from a dark studio apartment resembling a rabbit warren into the light, spacious and practical hub of the household. A large family room, large kitchen and breakfast room – opening out onto the garden – are complemented by the necessities of a large, luxurious house. A dumb waiter, a utility room, a laundry chute, a nanny's bedroom with doors to a sunken garden, and a separate bathroom complete the floor. The garage now gives easy access to two cars.

- the **entrance** from the garage, the **hallway** and the **stairs** up are all well configured, spacious and do not waste valuable floor space

- the **utility room** is sensibly located in the dark centre of the lower ground floor so as not to waste valuable window space – as the former apartments' utility rooms did

- the **nanny's bedroom** is a reasonable size, and very light thanks to the sunken garden that was reclaimed from the former earth fill

- the **bathroom** serves the nanny's room and the rest of the floor and, although small, is practical

- the **laundry chute** and **dumb waiter** serve all floors and add to the luxury and practicality of the home

- the **kitchen** is large and very well laid-out with a central island

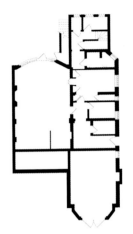

ORIGINAL LOWER GROUND FLOOR

KEY

BATHROOM

NANNY'S BEDROOM

HALLWAY

KITCHEN

RECEPTION ROOMS

SERVICES DUCT

STORAGE

UTILITY ROOM

- the **family room** is equally large and well appointed and has views and access to the garden

- the **breakfast room** flows from the kitchen and feels as if it is part of the garden thanks to a new 6m-high glazed wall on the rear extension with three doors that fold back completely to give access to the garden at lower ground level. Part of the breakfast area also has double head height, which adds further to the outdoor feel

REVISED LOWER GROUND FLOOR LAYOUT

FAMILY ROOM

DUMB WAITER

SERVICES RISER

LAUNDRY CHUTE

BOILER

SUNKEN GARDEN

0   5M

Ground floor becomes formal entertaining zone

The ground floor has been transformed from a two bedroom apartment into the formal entertaining space of the new family home. The double entrance lobby opens out onto a grand double staircase, lit from top to bottom by an 8 metre window; a media room, a formal dining room, a formal living room, a toilet and a study complete the floor.

ORIGINAL GROUND FLOOR

KEY

▨	BATHROOM
▨	HALLWAY
▨	RECEPTION ROOMS
▨	STORAGE
▨	SERVICES DUCT
▨	STUDY

SECTION THROUGH ALL FLOORS RUNNING FROM A TO B

A   B

REVISED GROUND FLOOR LAYOUT

FULL-HEIGHT
SHEET GLASS

A

VOID OVER
BREAKFAST
AREA

FORMAL
DINING

FORMAL
LIVING

DUMB
WAITER

SERVICES
RISER

LAUNDRY
CHUTE

MEDIA
ROOM

B

- the **entrance hall** and double staircase give a sense of maximum space and light, highlighted by the 8m window running the full height of the double staircase. The bespoke, contemporary-style staircase is the main feature and adds to the sense of space

- the **media room** is large and well laid out

- the formal **dining room** is flooded by light thanks to a sheet glass wall that overlooks the double-height breakfast area and the garden beyond. The dumb waiter serves the dining room. A door leads to:
  - the formal **living room** which is large and overlooks the garden.

  Another door leads back to the entrance hall with:
  - the **toilet** which is well proportioned
  - the **study** which is cosy but still a good size

0   5M

The sleeping floor with an award winning bathroom

The first floor has been transformed beyond recognition from the former first floor of the poorly appointed four-bedroom duplex. It is now the main sleeping floor for the family and makes maximum use of the space available. The grand double staircase leads up to a spacious landing and three well-appointed suites: the master suite complete with large bedroom, extensive bathroom facilities and two separate dressing areas; two children's bedrooms with en-suite facilities complete the floor. The master suite further benefits from the luxury of the dumb waiter opening out into its entrance lobby. The laundry chute also services this floor.

ORIGINAL FIRST FLOOR

- the **landing** is flooded with daylight from the 8m window that runs the height of the staircase. The landing is spacious and allows easy circulation

- the **master bedroom** is large, well appointed and private – thanks to its entrance lobby which secludes it from the rest of the house. The door to the master bedroom itself is a clever design: a pivot door that, when closed, gives the impression of being a continuous wall

- the **master bathroom's** 'wet' area is now housed on what was the terrace of the duplex's first floor. The two further areas of the master bathroom include double basins and dressing table; and a separate toilet and bidet. The latter is a far cry from the old-fashioned separate toilet. This design affords privacy without wasting space

- the two walk-in 'his' and 'hers' **dressing areas** are not only spacious and practical, but each closet benefits from natural daylight

- the **dumb waiter** makes the master suite truly self-contained and self-sufficient

- the **smaller children's bedroom** with en-suite is cosy and benefits from a good-sized built-in closet. The bathroom is small but has a bath, not just a shower

- the **larger children's bedroom** with en-suite has maximum light from the large bay window, excellent floor space and built-in closets. A good-size bathroom completes the suite

- the laundry chute makes life practical for the household

REVISED FIRST FLOOR

KEY

- DRESSING AREA
- EN-SUITE
- HALLWAY
- MASTER BEDROOM
- OTHER BEDROOMS
- SERVICES DUCT
- STORAGE

WET AREA

DUMB WAITER

SERVICES RISER

0   5M

The guest floor

The former second floor of the badly planned four-bedroom duplex has been transformed into the guest floor. Two large double bedrooms, each with fully glazed dormer windows, share a large bathroom. The household's storage requirements are met by two separate loft storage areas: the small loft off the bathroom, and the large loft off the landing.

SECTION RUNNING THROUGH ALL FLOORS FROM C TO D

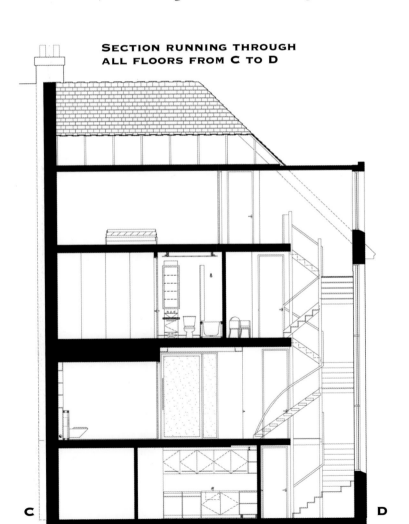

ORIGINAL SECOND FLOOR

KEY

BATHROOM

BEDROOMS

HALLWAY

STORAGE

SERVICES DUCT

STAGE 2 PLAN

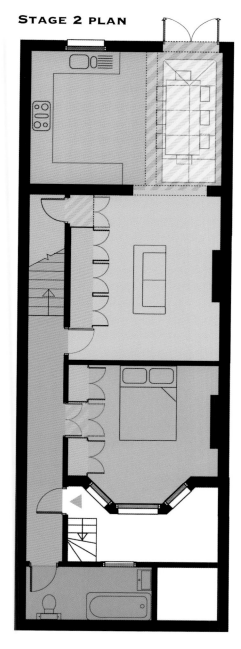

Taking it a step further

To open up the floor plan still further, another option would be to build the glazed extension as in Stage 1, but also to remove the corridor into the back room. This newly opened area could then house the spacious family room/home cinema and include ample storage space. The breakfast area would be sited in the side extension, with the kitchen making use of the existing plumbing facilities in the former bathroom/scullery area.

▌ the **bedroom** and **bathroom** would remain in the same positions as in Stage 1

▌ the glazed roof extension is carried out as in Stage 1, but the wall forming the corridor leading to the former back room is removed

▌ the **breakfast area** and **kitchen** occupy the new extension and former bathroom/scullery

▌ the **family room/home cinema**, complete with fireplace and ample storage, occupies the spacious area formerly taken up by the back room and corridor

▌ the **guest bedroom** and **bathroom** are in the same locations as in Stage 1

KEY

BATHROOM	LIVING AREA
BEDROOM	STORAGE
KITCHEN	UTILITY ROOM
HALLWAY	

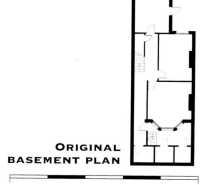

ORIGINAL BASEMENT PLAN

0   5M

*Structurally
more involved
but spatially
more rewarding*
The next step, in terms of
both investment and work
involved, would entail not
only building a glazed side
extension as shown on the previous pages but also
opening up the layout of the basement almost
completely. More structural work is required to
support the floors above, but this would certainly be
worthwhile if an open-plan feel is the desired effect.
This solution offers maximum light flow right
through the basement.

This option emphasizes the advantage the basement
has over the floor above. Steps down from street level
lead into the new kitchen area – isolated by a new
inner door – sited in the former bedroom and
corridor area. Some structural support is required
where the bedroom walls have been removed. The
utility room is sited in the converted coal hole. The
kitchen opens into the breakfast/dining area, which
opens into the family room/home cinema and toilet.

■ the side extension and former scullery house the **family
room/home cinema** with a **separate toilet**

■ all walls to the former back room have been removed and
supports installed. This now becomes the **breakfast/dining area**

■ the former bedroom becomes part of the new **open-plan
kitchen**. Though easily accessible from street level it is isolated
from the exterior by a **new inner door**

■ the hob is housed in the fireplace for a **farmhouse effect**

■ a **utility room** is sited in the former coal hole

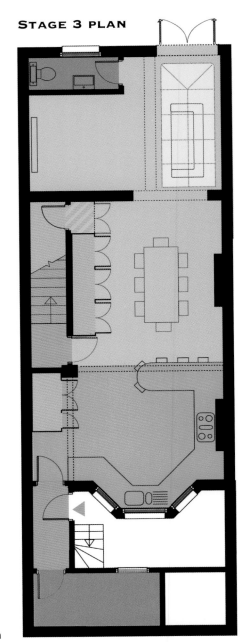

STAGE 3 PLAN

OPTIONAL PLAN

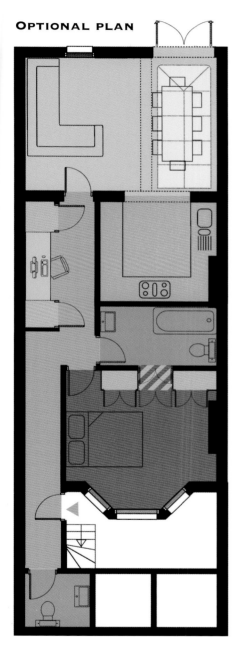

...*or as a separate apartment*

Transforming the basement into a separate home could involve similar changes to those in Stage 1, but the loss of the now redundant staircase leading up to the upper-ground floor means the welcome addition of space. A home office is now possible in the corridor, although without natural light. The bedroom is sited in the same position, but using the original door. This allows the bathroom – also accessible from the original corridor entrance – to become an en suite. To solve the problem of lack of daylight in the bathroom, a sandblasted panel could be included in the kitchen wall to allow light in from the rear. Another panel, above glazed double doors to the bedroom, could also bring light from the front window. Converting the coal cellar at the front means that an extra toilet can be sited here.

- the **glazed roof extension** houses the open-plan living/dining and kitchen areas

- the **bedroom** has a fireplace and double closets and remains in the same position as the former bedroom, but with a new entrance. Glazed doors allow light into the bathroom

- an **en-suite bathroom** is also accessed from the corridor

- a **home office** is sited where the stairs used to lead up to the ground floor

- a **toilet** is sited in the converted coal cellar for guests

KEY

■	BATHROOM	■	HALLWAY
■	EN-SUITE	■	LIVING AREA
■	BEDROOM	■	STORAGE
■	KITCHEN	■	UTILITY ROOM

ORIGINAL BASEMENT PLAN

0   5M

Going underground – something different to do with the garden

CONCEPT: PAULA ROBINSON DESIGN GROUP

This project took the upper ground and basement floors of a terraced house in its original configuration, as built in the 1900s. It had previously been divided from the upper floors and now had its own entrance from the communal corridor on the upper ground level.

It was reminiscent of all terraced houses with a front, middle and back room layout and an access corridor and staircase. Also typical was the open side return of the garden which brought light to the middle room. The garden to the rear was a good size, but was underutilized for most of the year. The high walls dividing the garden from adjoining properties meant careful maintenance was needed for it to look its best when it was in use.

The intention was to incorporate the garden area into the living space, creating a more contemporary feel which would then enable more suitable use of the existing rooms. This all had to be accomplished while still retaining some easy-to-use outdoor space.

Existing problems

▮ the individual rooms felt constrained and old fashioned and were not ideal in their layout

▮ the basement lacked light

▮ there was a shortage of accommodation

▮ the deep walled garden was rarely used

Objectives

▮ to create **additional living space** with a contemporary feel

▮ to bring **additional light** to the basement

▮ to make use of the **garden** as living space

▮ to retain some **low-maintenance** outdoor space

ORIGINAL BASEMENT AND UPPER GROUND FLOOR PLANS

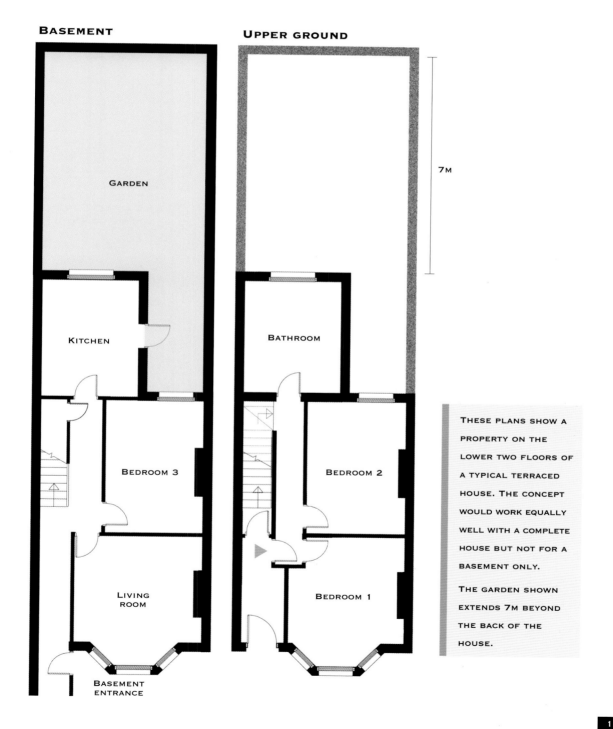

BASEMENT

GARDEN

KITCHEN

BEDROOM 3

LIVING ROOM

BASEMENT ENTRANCE

UPPER GROUND

7M

BATHROOM

BEDROOM 2

BEDROOM 1

THESE PLANS SHOW A PROPERTY ON THE LOWER TWO FLOORS OF A TYPICAL TERRACED HOUSE. THE CONCEPT WOULD WORK EQUALLY WELL WITH A COMPLETE HOUSE BUT NOT FOR A BASEMENT ONLY.

THE GARDEN SHOWN EXTENDS 7M BEYOND THE BACK OF THE HOUSE.

Your own private, tranquil view The design solution for the issue of 'too much garden, not enough luxury space' was to excavate the large garden and build a large underground extension for the master suite accommodation. Light is brought to both the original basement, and the new underground extension, by means of a light well. This involves creating an inner courtyard that brings light via floor-to-ceiling glass panels.

The original outdoor space is not lost – it has been moved up a floor where a low-maintenance paved terrace extends over the entire extension. This terrace is accessed via the upper ground floor and overlooks the inner courtyard below.

Uses of the other rooms on the ground floor and basement can be altered according to personal taste but have not been suggested here as the main focus is on the underground area.

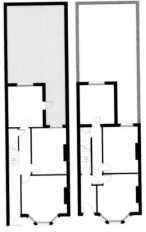

ORIGINAL BASEMENT AND UPPER GROUND FLOOR PLANS

KEY

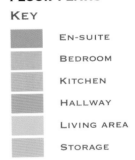

EN-SUITE

BEDROOM

KITCHEN

HALLWAY

LIVING AREA

STORAGE

- the outer scullery wall has been removed and **steel beams** installed to support the walls above

- this enabled the **side return** to be annexed into the living space

- the **garden** has been excavated to create a **master suite** complete with dressing area, bedroom and bathroom (with separate shower). All of which overlook:
  - an **inner courtyard** viewed through floor-to-ceiling glass walls and accessible through glazed doors from the bedroom

- use of the **living areas** in the rest of the property can be tailored to personal use, so long as the kitchen is isolated for fire safety

- **double doors** replace the window in the middle room on the upper floor and steps lead down to:
  - a **large terrace** which extends the length and width of the new space below and replaces the original garden as the house's outdoor space. It overlooks the inner courtyard below. This area requires little maintenance save watering tubs of plants in dry weather

REVISED LAYOUT

BASEMENT

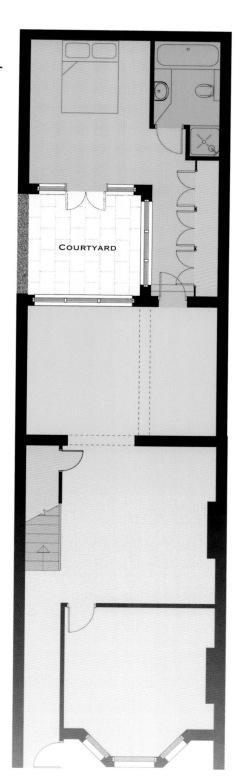

COURTYARD

UPPER GROUND

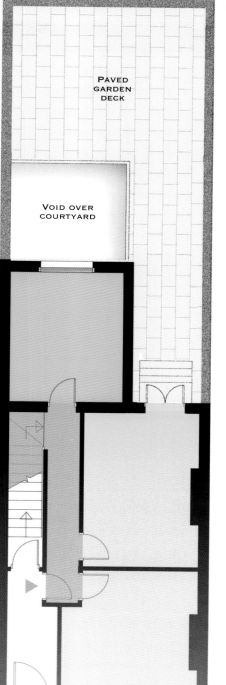

PAVED GARDEN DECK

VOID OVER COURTYARD

0   5M

Creating three different outdoor areas

Alternatively, the courtyard could be placed on the right-hand side of the plan, offering the ability to create three individual outdoor areas instead of just two.

The new external doors from the middle room on the upper ground could open onto a decked area overlooking the courtyard. Access to the terraced area would then be through the back room, via new external doors there.

Once again, as the accent here is on the garden area, no changes have been shown to the existing internal space. A number of options which would work in conjunction are shown in the previous project (see pages 184–9).

The ability to apply this concept is largely dependent on the height of the existing garden walls or – put another way – the depth of the existing garden. If the level of a terrace built on top of the new space means neighbours could be overlooked, planning objections would arise. The depth of the excavation would be dictated by the depth of boundary foundations. If higher or deeper walls are needed, consultation and co-operation with neighbours could benefit all parties as they would have the opportunity to develop their properties in a similar way.

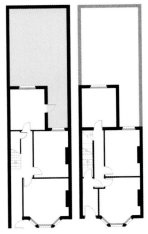

ORIGINAL LOWER AND UPPER GROUND FLOORS

KEY

	EN-SUITE
	BEDROOM
	KITCHEN
	HALLWAY
	LIVING AREA
	STORAGE

- **courtyard** switches to right-hand side of plan

- this enables creation of **additional decked area** overlooking courtyard

- terrace now accessed through new external doors leading from back room

- see previous project (pages 184-9) for options on revised layouts for existing **internal living space**

- **height of existing walls** and **depth of foundations** may limit or prevent use of this concept. Co-operation from neighbours may be essential

OPTIONAL LAYOUT

BASEMENT

C

COURTYARD

B — — — — — A

SECTION

FROM A TO B, AS VIEWED FROM C

A

B

GARDEN WALL ABOVE TERRACE

FLOORS OF MAIN STRUCTURE

UPPER GROUND

PAVED GARDEN DECK

VOID OVER COURTYARD

DECKED AREA

0   5M

Maximizing usable loft space

ARCHITECT: UV ARCHITECTS

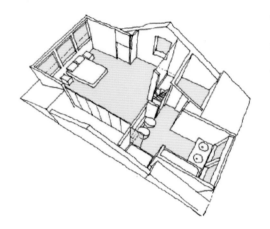

This property had a loft conversion carried out in the 1980s, but the resulting space was less than practical in a number of ways. The head height in the loft created restrictions for the bed's position, and moving around the space felt constrained. The staircase to the loft was narrow, thereby making access feel restricted and uncomfortable. The staircase's position also created problems on the floor below, as it rose from a position that interfered with a planned new shower room on that floor. The storage area was rarely used. The sloping roof made it virtually impossible to reach items placed at the very back of the storage space. The overall result was a loft conversion that was rarely used because it was neither practical nor comfortable.

Existing problems

- the existing **staircase** to the loft area was narrow and badly positioned within the space – and for the floor below

- the **head height** created problems for positioning a double bed

- the **bathroom** benefited from a window, but its layout and position within the loft space were less than ideal

- the **storage space** was almost unusable because of the roof's slope

ORIGINAL
FLOOR PLAN

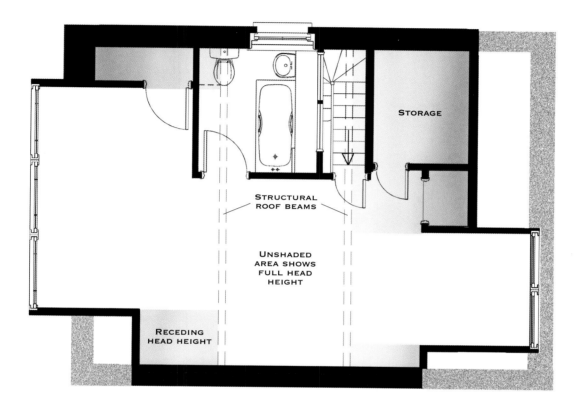

STORAGE

STRUCTURAL
ROOF BEAMS

UNSHADED
AREA SHOWS
FULL HEAD
HEIGHT

RECEDING
HEAD HEIGHT

Objectives

▮ to create a new, practical bedroom suite with well positioned bed and bathroom

▮ to create a new shower room for the floor below

▮ to reposition the staircase to give good access to

the new bedroom suite and also fit into the plan for the floor below

▮ to make maximum use of full head height

▮ to create accessible storage space

New staircase key to solving the problem

The new bedroom suite is now accessed by a wide staircase that has been re-sited on the opposite side of the property. The new position means it makes use of maximum head height where it reaches the loft. It gives a sense of space and volume to the area and sets the tone for the new suite, which no longer feels like a badly executed loft conversion. Development of the floor below was no longer hampered by the old staircase's position.

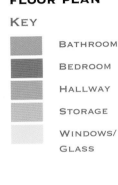

ORIGINAL FLOOR PLAN

KEY

BATHROOM

BEDROOM

HALLWAY

STORAGE

WINDOWS/ GLASS

3D PLAN

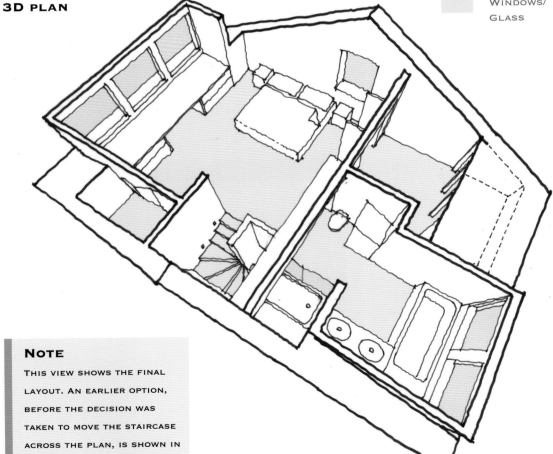

NOTE

THIS VIEW SHOWS THE FINAL LAYOUT. AN EARLIER OPTION, BEFORE THE DECISION WAS TAKEN TO MOVE THE STAIRCASE ACROSS THE PLAN, IS SHOWN IN THE IMAGE ON PAGE 196.

■ the **staircase** is now wide and well positioned

■ the **bedroom** is practical, with a built-in dressing table beneath the windows and built-in double wardrobes opposite the bed

■ the **bathroom** has a bath, separate shower and double-basin vanity unit and a storage cupboard. The layout gives a good sense of space and

separates the toilet nicely from the main part of the room. A sliding door to the bathroom maximizes the sense of space

■ by gaining floor space from the old staircase, more of the **storage room** now has good head height, making it a more accessible, practical area. Double doors are used to minimize space loss

THE FINISHED LOFT PLAN

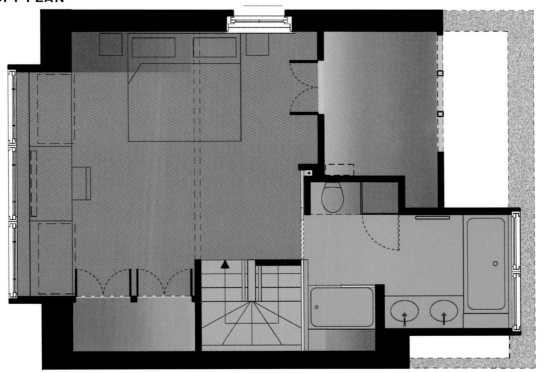

0   5M

ROOM-BY-ROOM SPACE

Innovative solutions for activity-specific areas

*R*e-shaping our homes to meet our evolving needs places many constraints on us, no matter how vivid our imagination or large our budget. We may design our homes around the principles of flexible space – altering our rooms at the touch of a button – but, like it or not, certain spaces will remain activity-specific by necessity. The kitchen and the bathroom are the front-runners in this category. Living, dining, working and sleeping areas can easily be adapted to our need for change, but the services that the kitchen and bathroom require will keep them firmly in their place for a while to come.

Deploying the tricks of shape and colour that we discussed in High-Performance Space can help to disguise the solid permanence of kitchens and bathrooms. Understanding the role that these activity-specific areas play in our lives, and identifying what changes we need to make for them to serve us better, will help us as we plan homes to carry us easily into the future.

We tend to take these activity-specific rooms for granted in their present form and to forget that they have evolved – and will continue to do so. To get a sense of how to plan these areas so that they will adapt to suit our changing needs, it is first worth glancing over our shoulder to see how they have evolved beyond all recognition from their modest beginnings.

Looking back

Kitchens: from understudy to star

The kitchen has undergone some of the most striking changes in keeping with our evolving needs. It started out as an outbuilding in medieval times, for safety reasons, but gradually worked its way indoors to end up in the heart of the home by the late 20th century. Many homes now have the kitchen as part of the 'family room', or at least in an area that allows the cook to feel part of the household instead of shut away from it.

Kitchens were once areas rarely seen by anyone other than the servants, and their design had everything to do with practicality and nothing to do with aesthetics. When servants became the exception rather than the rule and the lady of the house took over in the kitchen, women's emancipation led to the design-conscious kitchen. It had double criteria to fulfil: at once pleasing to her and practical. As such, 20th-century kitchen design became a tribute to a model known as the 'scientific management of the home'. The kitchen's structure – and the way it was run – was actually based on a variation of the public factory model. The only problem with this scientific model was the fact that working on a production line is one thing, but attempting to incorporate production line principles into the home is quite another. Clinical starkness, with form following function, was the ideal, but many homes designed in this way lacked soul. Nowhere was this better illustrated than in the kitchen.

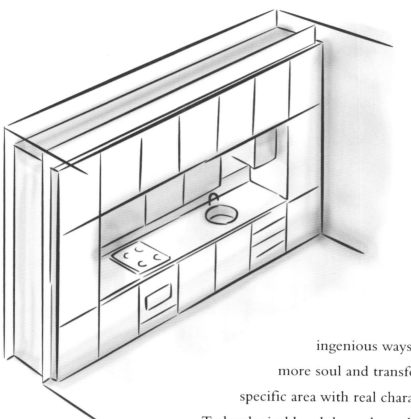

THE NEXT STEP FOR THE KITCHEN

This leaves us with the big question: just how will the kitchen evolve now? Will we cling to the production-line model as everything becomes more automated and we have less time on our hands?

Or will we find ingenious ways to give the kitchen more soul and transform it into an activity-specific area with real character beyond its purpose? Technological breakthroughs and our growing need for flexibility in our homes may give us funky, mobile kitchens – just for starters!

Bathrooms: from necessity to luxury

Over to another activity-specific area: the bathroom. In the castles and manor houses of the medieval West, all ablutions were conducted indoors in garde-robes – vertical passageways that ran across a corner of the building, equipped with wooden seats, which drained into the moat or cesspool – and in portable slipper baths placed in front of the bedroom fire.

By the 18th century, the 'houses of office' – as they were known – had been moved out into the garden, along with the Roman-inspired cold plunge pools, with hot showers beside them. It was not until the 20th century that the built-in bathroom as we know it became standard.

In the 21st century we seem to be approaching bathing in two quite distinct ways, and many homes are starting to reflect this altered awareness.

TECHNO-CLINICAL BATHING

On the one hand, we have the streamlined, rational bathroom associated with necessity, cleanliness and practicality – the Japanese have taken this one clinical step further than us with their 'car-wash'-style toilet.

Technology is beginning to offer some space-age concepts for the gadget-mad amongst us. Take for instance the user-ID-specific shower rooms that offer each family member a completely tailor-made package. Each user is identified on entry by a hand imprint reading and everything within the shower room then adjusts accordingly: shower head height, water temperature and pressure, and so forth. And, to give the true 'Big Brother is watching you' feel, how about a mirror that scans heart rate, temperature and any number of other vital daily statistics to keep you healthy?

This rational bathroom is reminiscent of the factory production line approach to the kitchen, functional and gadget-friendly – but is it relaxing and uplifting?

LEISURE BATHING

Which brings us neatly to the second approach to bathing: the leisure-bathing area. This is a space – either public or private – completely devoted to the therapeutic effects of water. The Romans first introduced us to this idea with their thermae, and their example was closely followed throughout the centuries by public spas.

The 20th century saw the basics of the concept introduced into the home with the Jacuzzi and the hot tub, but these never quite managed to encapsulate the healing and therapeutic atmosphere of a spa.

WET ROOMS: FAD OR FRONT RUNNER?

Wet rooms have created quite a stir in recent times. Are they an investment worth making in your home or will they date and become obsolete?

A wet room can be a wonderful camouflage for the fact that the property lacks a bath (an important feature for a lot of people). Indeed, state-of-the-art wet rooms can be a great selling point.

It is sensible to consider underfloor heating when

installing a wet room, a feature that will not only be pleasant underfoot in winter but also practical in drying off the floor surface rapidly once the water has drained away.

THE WAY FORWARD

Ultimately, will our bathrooms be clinical conveyor belts or mini spas? Or a combination of both? Will bathrooms become mobile or remain one of the few fixed areas in the home?

With the help of technology and our deeper understanding of the psychological and spiritual effects that our surroundings have on us, will we start to create bathing areas that are truly adaptable to our many different needs?

Back to the drawing board

Cooking and bathing areas will remain as fixed areas in our otherwise flexible homes for the foreseeable future, mainly for reasons of safety and privacy. As such, they can have a character all of their own, quite distinct from the rest of the home.

Adding a little fire

Gone are the days when you could enjoy the luxury of a fire only if you were lucky enough to have a property with a working chimney breast and/or a gas supply. Today, anyone can have a fire, wherever they choose in their property – in the kitchen, the bathroom or wherever whim dictates. Better still, the fuss, mess and general commotion of installation are all yesterday's news.

What you will be installing these days, though, will not give you a traditional log-burning fire – you might have to resort to the country estate for that! These are modern fires, reflective of a new sense of style and design and a far cry from the traditional grate and firedogs framed by an elaborate mantelpiece.

Think minimal. Think hole in the wall. Think pebbles. Think stylish and simple. Most importantly, think low-maintenance.

The beauty of inset fires is that they can be positioned wherever you like. Often you will see them set low down, close to the floor – an easy and cost-effective way of adapting an existing opening. But they are equally striking set higher up the wall. It all depends on your ceiling height, the size of the room and the effect that you are trying to create.

Currently, by far the easiest and least expensive option is to choose a gel flame fire over a gas fire. With a gas fire, you not only need a gas supply to be run to your chosen location, but also adequate ventilation, which can limit your options on positioning. The only drawback with gel flame fires is that you do need to replace the burning gel cans – the source of the flame – on a regular basis. But the upside is that you can install the fire of your choice in the location of your choice.

Not forgetting the entrance hall

Finally, we need to turn our attention to one other area that, although not truly activity-specific, is still somewhat fixed within its own confines: the entrance hall. While the grand hall used to be a design statement, these days it seems to be an area that we would rather do without, although fire regulations in Britain require us to include it in our plans.

What to do with the entrance hall to make it blend in with the rest of the property?

AN EASY OPTION

Mirroring the wall immediately opposite the entrance door can create an interesting feature. It is much more interesting to be greeted by a wall of mirror that reflects colour and light from the wall opposite than to be confronted by a plain, solid wall. Mirror suggests that the property has some life and character. A plain wall is just boring, no matter how much you may try to convince yourself that it's somehow very Tate Modern!

ADD COLOUR

If you go a step further and add dramatic colour to the mirrored hall, this will help to confuse the eye as to the actual size of the hall – which can often be small and pokey.

Most people are naturally wary of using strong colours in small spaces. They are far more comfortable opting for light colours wherever possible, believing that this will make the space feel larger.

Most light shades – including all whites and creams – only highlight the exact contours of the room, drawing attention to the actual size and the obvious lack of space.

Dark colours, especially when they are also applied to ceilings, blur the boundaries, like a soft-focus photograph.

ADD AN ARCHITECTURAL NOTE

Another solution, with a more architectural feel, is to take the floor-to-ceiling mirrored wall one step further. Instead of covering the wall in mirror, first fit it with equally spaced floor-to-ceiling battens, painted to match the walls, woodwork and ceiling. Then fit mirror sections, again floor to ceiling, between the painted battens. The effect is very eye-catching and succeeds in altering the sense of available space. As you walk into the hall you have the feeling that there is an area just beyond the architectural battens, thereby creating the illusion that the hallway is much wider than it really is.

If your budget and the floor structure allow, consider floor-mounted lights, as they can create a stunning and unexpected look, coupled with pinpricks of overhead light from the ceiling.

Remember that the art of amazing halls lies in simplicity, both of line and detail. Less is definitely more.

Seamless period space

ARCHITECT: HUGH BROUGHTON

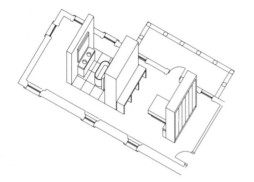

This property was once the elegant ballroom of a 19th century manor house set in a picturesque, rolling landscape. It even had the façade of an 18th-century property, added after the latter was dismantled from a nearby valley and carried, stone by stone, up to its new position.

The ballroom's beauty and style were completely lost in the 1920s, when utilitarian space became more important than ballrooms. A false, lowered ceiling was installed, period features were lost, and the space was divided up into a series of small rooms.

Its location, set at the south end of the historic house it once served, was perhaps its last remaining advantage.

Existing problems

- the entire space was given over to cramped, low-ceilinged rooms

- the light from the south-facing location was minimized by the room divisions and low ceilings

- while chimney breasts remained, the fireplace and mantle had been stripped out, leaving a bare monolith encroaching on the room

Objectives

- to restore the space to some of its former glory, complete with its original **sense of space** and volume

- to give the space a new **modern identity** as a bedchamber to contrast with its surroundings

- the new bedchamber had to include **sleeping, bathing, dressing** and **sitting areas**

ORIGINAL
FLOOR PLAN

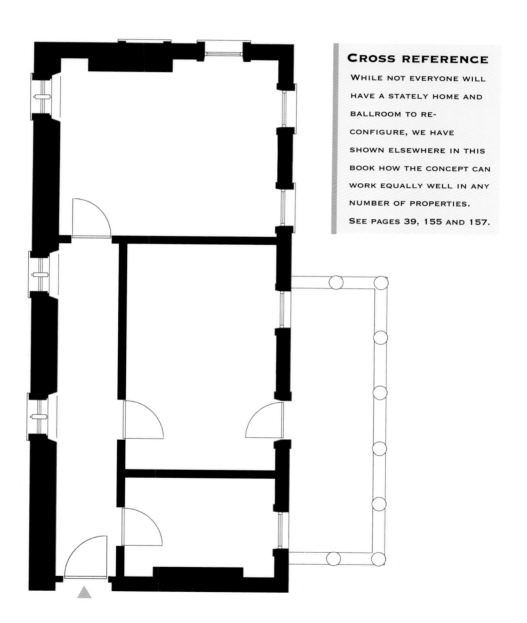

CROSS REFERENCE

WHILE NOT EVERYONE WILL
HAVE A STATELY HOME AND
BALLROOM TO RE-
CONFIGURE, WE HAVE
SHOWN ELSEWHERE IN THIS
BOOK HOW THE CONCEPT CAN
WORK EQUALLY WELL IN ANY
NUMBER OF PROPERTIES.
SEE PAGES 39, 155 AND 157.

Your own private waltz

The former ballroom's new incarnation as a bedchamber has a wonderful flow to it, reminiscent of the sweeping circle of a waltz around a ballroom. The new bedchamber is divided into sleeping, bathing and sitting areas by three central 'accommodation pods'. These create a contemporary contrast to the traditional setting. They appear as solid blocks without interrupting the sense of flow of the new space.

ORIGINAL FLOOR PLAN

KEY

▣	BATHROOM
▣	BEDROOM
▣	HALLWAY
▣	LIVING AREA
▣	STORAGE

ISOMETRIC VIEW

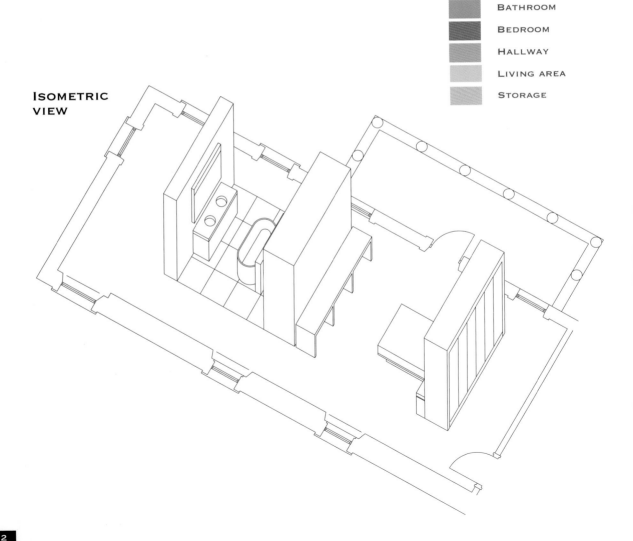

REVISED FLOOR PLAN

■ the **entrance** gives easy access to the sleeping, bathing and sitting areas in a flowing, unrestricted manner

■ the **sleeping area** is created by the first pod, which serves the dual purpose of closets on one side and bedhead for the sleeping area on the other

■ the **bathing area** is created by the second pod, which serves as the back of the dressing table on the sleeping area side, and houses the toilet and shower cubicle on the bathing area side. The bath takes centre stage, flanked by a plinth that supports the towel rails. The third pod serves as the wall for the double basin vanity unit on the bathing area side, with:

– the **sitting area's** bookshelves on the other side of the third pod

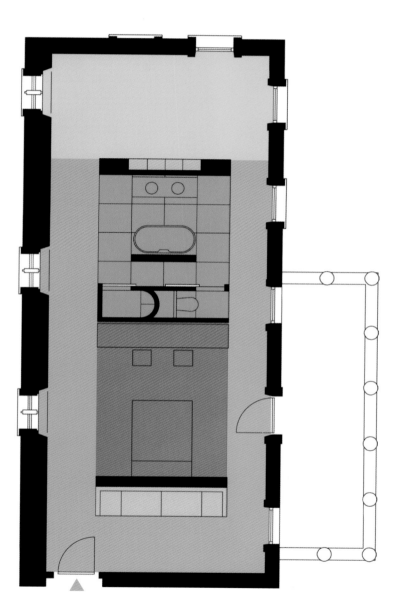

ALTHOUGH THIS LAYOUT DOES NOT INCORPORATE COOKING FACILITIES, MOST BACHELOR PADS WILL HAVE A SEPARATE BATHROOM, WHICH COULD BE REPLACED BY A KITCHENETTE, THUS CREATING A SELF-CONTAINED ENVIRONMENT.

O   5M

Storage within a stone's throw

CONCEPT: PAULA ROBINSON DESIGN GROUP

This bedroom was short on most things, including space, light, storage and character. The client wanted a room that would be reminiscent of his Greek heritage and that would prove both comfortable and inspirational.

A 'stone room' was created with a raised bed platform designed to look like an old stone wall. The 'stepped wall' unit doubles as headboard on one side and closet space on the other – creating a dressing area between the unit and the window. Flush floor-to-ceiling storage lines the wall around the window, with a window seat between. All walls are specialist-painted to match the stone clad bed platform.

Objectives

- to create the optical illusion of space in a cramped bedroom

- to create a bedroom with separate sleeping area and dressing area

- to give maximum closet and storage space

- to create an unusual room in keeping with the client's Greek origins

Solutions

- a 'stone' bedroom was created to mimic an **old Greek wall**

- a **bed platform** was built and tiled in tumbled stone to house the mattress in a recess – to keep it from moving. Space was left at the foot of the

platform as access to the far side of the bed

- large **storage drawers** open under the platform

- the stepped stone wall is for **mood lighting** and additional usable surfaces

- it also serves as **headboard** on one side, and **closets** on the other

- this creates a **separate dressing area** between the stone wall and the window

- floor-to-ceiling **storage** units flank the window, creating a window seat above the built-in radiator

- all walls and window storage units had a **specialist stone paint effect** applied to match the **real stone** of the bed platform

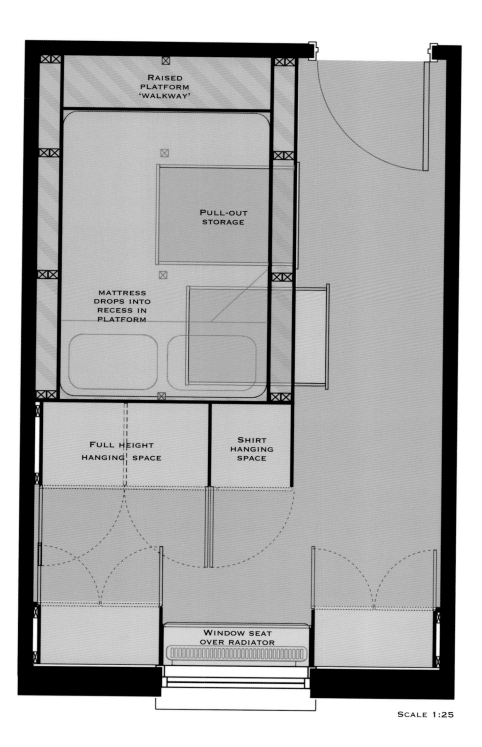

RAISED
PLATFORM
'WALKWAY'

PULL-OUT
STORAGE

MATTRESS
DROPS INTO
RECESS IN
PLATFORM

FULL HEIGHT
HANGING SPACE

SHIRT
HANGING
SPACE

WINDOW SEAT
OVER RADIATOR

SCALE 1:25

A room within a room

DESIGNER: PAULA ROBINSON DESIGN GROUP

This master bedroom with en-suite bathroom originally had two major problems. It had no closets or storage space and it felt claustrophobic with a double bed in any position other than immediately under the window. This did not leave any room for bedside units or further storage in the room.

It was necessary to create an optical illusion to give a sense of space where actually there was very little. The design solution took the form of an arched alcove bed with built-in storage. Aesthetics and practicalities were thus taken care of in one. The room assumed a Santa Fe theme, with the alcove bed being rough-plastered to create the desired effect. The bedroom felt larger and uncluttered thanks to the added storage.

Objectives

- to make the **bedroom** feel inviting and cosy, instead of cramped and oppressive

- to create additional **storage space**

- to include **mood/task lighting** and an unobtrusive housing space for a television

- to create **closet** space

Solutions

- a Santa Fe-style arched **bed alcove** was built and rough-plastered to make the bedroom feel cosy and to create the optical illusion of space

- the alcove includes deep **storage drawers** facing into the room

- within the alcove, **lighting** and useful **recesses** and surfaces are provided by a deep, stepped bedhead

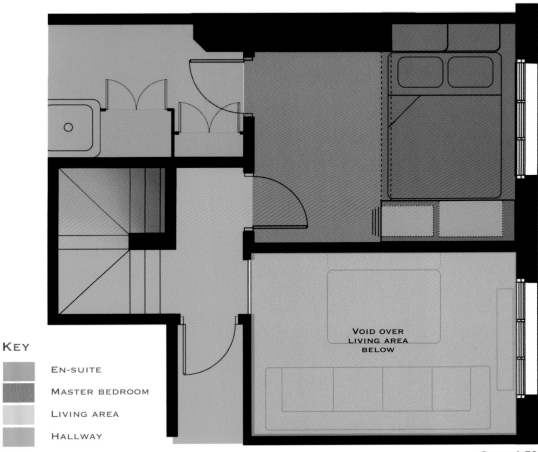

KEY

EN-SUITE

MASTER BEDROOM

LIVING AREA

HALLWAY

VOID OVER
LIVING AREA
BELOW

SCALE 1:50

- the television is concealed in the matching stepped structure at the foot of the bed

- **closet** storage has been introduced in an underutilized area of the en-suite bathroom

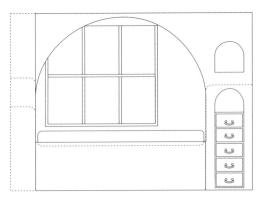

THE STEPPED SHAPE OF THE BEDHEAD ALLOWS FOR PLACING MOOD/TASK LIGHTING. THE CORRESPONDING AREA OF THE BED BASE CONCEALS THE TELEVISION FROM VIEW OTHER THAN FROM THE BED ITSELF.

Two bathrooms sharing a bedroom

ARCHITECT: UV ARCHITECTS

Creating an extra bathroom in a home without reducing the number of bedrooms – or creating major upheaval – is a frequent problem for city dwellers living in constricted properties. This house was a classic example: it was small and only had two bedrooms with the one bathroom located on a half-landing. The family needed a third bedroom, and the master bedroom had to have an en-suite facility.

The solution to bedroom space was solved by converting the loft into a third bedroom. Here we focus on how the original bathroom was turned into a small bedroom and the former second bedroom into two bathrooms: one being the family bathroom, the other being the small en-suite shower room for the master bedroom.

The resulting two bathrooms are an unusual shape, but this adds to their character and appeal. Placing the double-ended bath at an angle allowed easy access to the room without encroaching on the toilet bowl. The en-suite, while compact, serves its purpose and steals space – through the dividing wall – from the bedroom's cupboard for its own storage.

Objectives

- to create an additional bedroom and an en-suite bathroom without compromising the lower ground and ground floors

- to remodel the first floor to provide a family bathroom and en-suite for the master bedroom

- to restrict work to the interior to avoid delays inherent with planning permission for external works

Solutions

- former bedroom two was transformed into two separate areas:
  - a small but adequate **en-suite shower room** for the master bedroom and
  - a **family bathroom** that is spacious and well appointed. Its proximity to the master bedroom means the lack of a bath in the en-suite facility is less of a problem

KEY

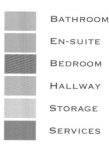

BATHROOM

EN-SUITE

BEDROOM

HALLWAY

STORAGE

SERVICES

SCALE 1:50

Washing your bathroom with light

ARCHITECT: JONATHAN CLARK

Creating a practical bathroom that feels spacious and inviting in a restrictive space can be difficult, especially if there is no window to add a sense of depth and light.

Incorporating good storage can compromise the sense of space still further.

The solution is to play with levels and light to create a bathroom that is not claustrophobic. A step up onto a bath platform immediately creates a sense of luxury, especially if the underside of the platform is lit to give the illusion that it is floating. The same idea is used with the storage units above the bath and basins: a wash of light above and below each lends another dimension to the space. Using an opaque glass panel at one end of the bath brings daylight from the next-door room without compromising privacy.

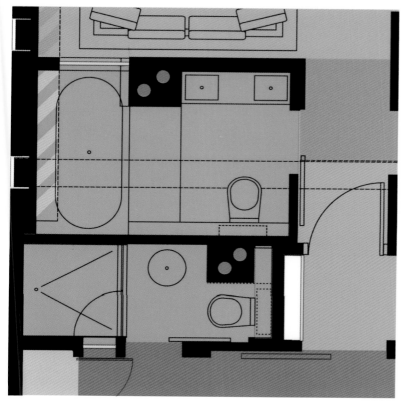

KEY

■ BATHROOM
■ EN-SUITE
■ MASTER BEDROOM
■ HALL
■ LIVING AREA
■ STORAGE
■ UTILITY DUCT
■ WINDOW/GLASS

SCALE 1:80

Objectives

■ to create a luxury bathroom within a restrictive, windowless space

■ to compensate for the lack of natural daylight

■ to maximize the sense of space within the bathroom

■ to create maximum storage space

Solutions

■ a **sliding bathroom door** reduces space loss within the room itself and sets the contemporary tone of the space

■ **concealed lighting** beneath a bath platform makes both the platform and the bath appear to float

■ **storage cabinets** above the bath and basins cover the practical issues, and clever concealed lighting above and below each unit again makes them appear to float

■ the washes of light help to confuse the eye as to the exact size of the bathroom

■ an **etched glass panel** to the right of the bath brings natural daylight in from the next room, without compromising privacy

■ each surface slides and blends into another, creating diversification and interest

Giving width to narrow wet room

DESIGNER: PAULA ROBINSON DESIGN GROUP

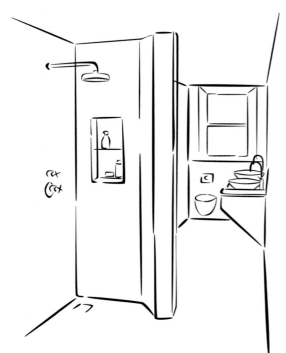

The area used for this bathroom – which led off the master suite – offered plenty of space and light, but the room was long and narrow. To give a feeling of depth, limestone and mirrors were used throughout. The entire wall opposite the door was mirrored – from worksurface height to ceiling – with tiles below this line.

A bevel-based, wall-mounted washplane appeared to float above the floor, giving an illusion of width. This was also clad in limestone, but with tinted maple trim and two wooden, surface-mounted basins, which became the room's only contrast to the limestone.

The wet area's wall gave a feeling of division between vanity and bathing areas. With the wall-hung toilet, this became the only interruption to the flow of the floor space, thus enhancing the feeling of width.

Objectives

- to create a luxury master bathroom that included a separate shower

- to camouflage the room's long, narrow shape

- to create two distinct but not totally separate areas

- to ensure that the bathroom felt warm and dry underfoot

Solutions

- the floor and all the walls were tiled in **limestone,** with **mirror** running the entire length of one wall – from worksurface height to ceiling

- a **washplane** was built and tiled in limestone, providing a large worksurface, but tapering off at an angle before reaching the floor. This prevented the visual narrowing of the floor space – as would have occurred with a traditional vanity unit

- wooden, surface-mounted **basins** contrast with the limestone

- matching wooden lids open to reveal **storage** below

- a void was left behind the mirrored wall. This enabled full-height **cabinets** with push catches to be concealed behind the washplane, their doors running flush with the rest of the mirror plane

- a **wet area** wall to deflect spray from the entranceway also served to break up the narrow passage effect between basins and bath

- **underfloor heating** was installed to keep the bathroom dry and warm underfoot

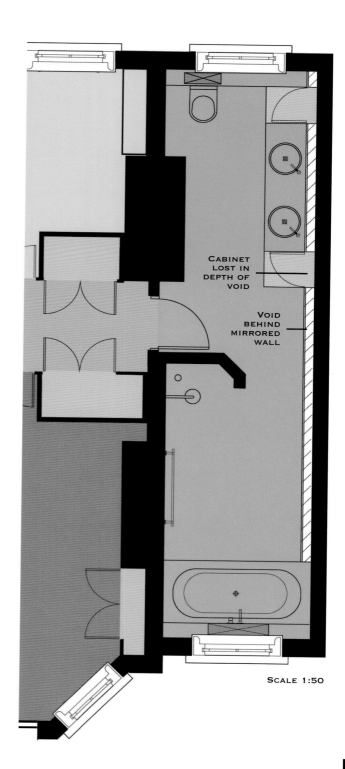

CABINET LOST IN DEPTH OF VOID

VOID BEHIND MIRRORED WALL

SCALE 1:50

KEY

	BATHROOM
	BEDROOM
	HALLWAY
	STORAGE
	STUDY
	SERVICE ACCESS

A bathroom with a view

ARCHITECT: SPENCE HARRIS HOGAN

We are accustomed to seeing skylights and lightwells used in living and sleeping areas to bring additional light and interest to darker spaces. Using skylights in bathrooms can bring a fine sense of outdoor space, especially if a skylight is located above a shower.

This bathroom was sited on the ground floor of a two storey property. The skylight is round to mirror the shape of the shower itself. The unusual aspect of this skylight is that it is located in the decking of the roof terrace above – forming a very large peep-hole!

The rest of this spacious bathroom complements the circular shower: a double-ended bath in an alcove, a toilet and bidet beneath the window squaring off the angle of the room created by the shape of the building's outer wall, and a large vanity unit with double round basins mirroring the shape of the shower.

The shower cubicle built into the bedroom next door creates the bath's alcove. This, together with a communal toilet on this floor, completed facilities for this third bedroom, while the second bedroom also benefited from an en-suite.

KEY

▉	BATHROOM
▉	BEDROOM
▉	MASTER BEDROOM
▉	HALLWAY
▉	STORAGE

Objectives

▮ to create a spacious master bathroom

▮ to bring additional light into the bathroom

▮ to create an unusual shower cubicle

▮ to create additional bathing facilities for the adjacent bedroom

Solutions

▮ the focal point of the master bathroom is a circular **corner shower** with a round **skylight** immediately above. The skylight brings not only additional daylight and a view of the sky into the bathroom, but also a cheeky view from the terrace above directly down into the shower

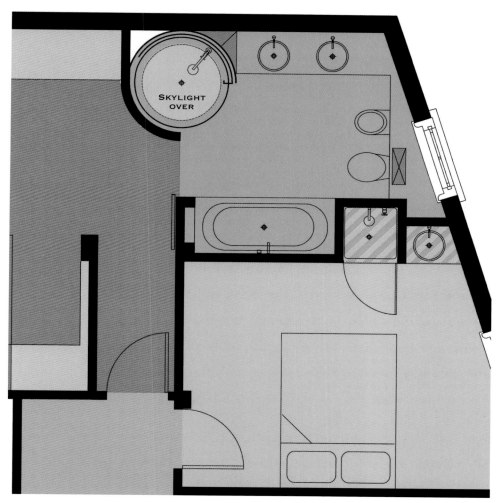

SKYLIGHT
OVER

SCALE 1:50

- the **double-ended bath** fits into an alcove created by the design of a shower cubicle in the next door bedroom

- a large **vanity unit** has **two round basins**, mirroring the shape of the shower and skylight

- the bathroom is contemporary in style, being open plan to the master bedroom

- the shape of the shower cubicle also adds to the master bedroom by providing a curved wall to the bedroom

A feeling of space in a tiny bachelor bathroom

ARCHITECT: JONATHAN CLARK

Restyling a small bachelor bathroom with no window into a fully functioning, aesthetically pleasing bathroom – with a sense of space – can be a challenge. Add to this the restrictions of having to use and work around the building's existing service ducts and the problem is compounded.

Advantage was taken of the unusual layout of this bathroom. The area immediately opposite the door is empty and draws the eye to the curved wall, giving an initial illusion of space within. The main working area of the bathroom is restricted to the rear of the room, with a large feature bath and shower as the focal point. The shower doors slide out from either side of the bath, allowing them to blend into the space while still defining it. A fixed glass panel would have drawn unnecessary attention to itself.

Daylight is brought in from the hallway through a half-height etched glass panel at one end of the bath, and from the entrance, which has a similarly glazed pivoting door.

Objectives

■ to completely refit the bathroom using the existing service ducts and within the original space

■ to leave enough working space in the room despite the constricted layout of the services

■ to include a bath and a high-performance shower

Solutions

■ the **entrance** to the bathroom feels spacious thanks to an empty 'drying off space' immediately opposite the door, enhanced by a curved wall

■ the position of the **toilet** gives it a sense of separation from the rest of the bathroom. It does not encroach on the main space

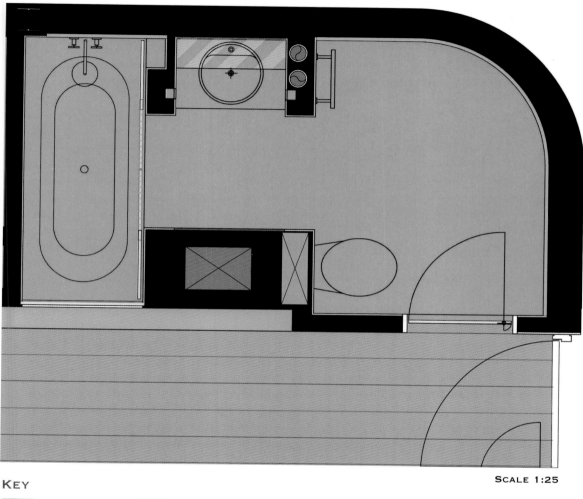

KEY

BATHROOM   MIRROR   STORAGE

ETCHED GLASS   MOSAIC   TILES

HALLWAY   SERVICES DUCT

■ the building's bulky utility duct behind the toilet is turned to advantage by the creation of a similar width vanity unit opposite, balancing it out and leading the eye towards the focal area:

■ the enclosed **bath** with **shower**. The two panels slide across symmetrically from either side of the

bath to provide the shower screen, giving the bath an unusual feature while still blending into the room

■ the bath, toilet and vanity units form a cohesive whole rather than the more standard separate pieces. This adds to the overall feeling of space and depth

A symmetrical bathing experience

ARCHITECT: JONATHAN CLARK

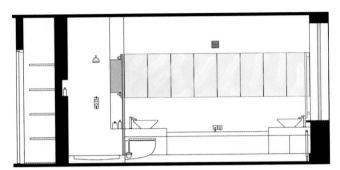

The design of this bathroom in a former bedroom was based on symmetry and balance – and on creating an unusual feature. We have all grown accustomed to the standard vanity unit with double basins in luxury bathrooms. Separating the two basins with the bath between them is not only novel, but works very well aesthetically. The bath and vanity units flow together with good clean lines instead of appearing as two separate boxy items in the bathroom.

Double doors opening directly opposite the bath give a grand entrance and view. They open back onto the walls, maximizing the sense of space in the room. The toilet is centred on the wall between two windows, directly opposite. The shower cubicle occupies the original entrance to the room. Unusually, this allows its inclusion without it encroaching on the floorspace of the bathroom.

Objectives

- to create a well balanced, symmetrical bathroom

- to create an unusual feature and focal point

- to utilize the room's corridor entrance, without compromising the symmetry of the new bathroom

- to create additional storage

Solutions

- **double doors** fold completely back and centre on the bathroom's focal point:

- a **double-basin** vanity unit separated by the double-ended bath

- a **shower cubicle** takes up the redundant space of the former corridor entrance, thus maintaining the

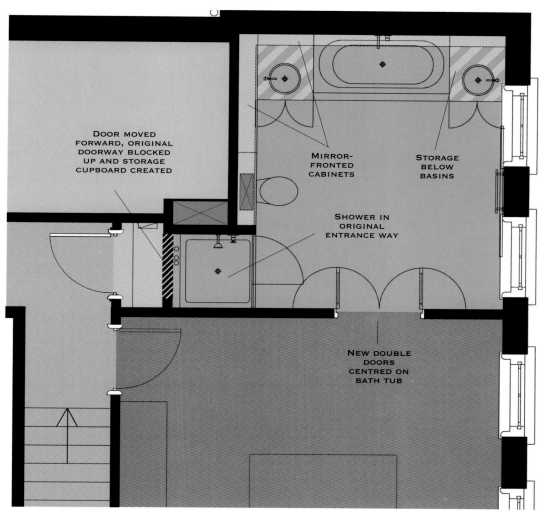

DOOR MOVED
FORWARD, ORIGINAL
DOORWAY BLOCKED
UP AND STORAGE
CUPBOARD CREATED

MIRROR-
FRONTED
CABINETS

STORAGE
BELOW
BASINS

SHOWER IN
ORIGINAL
ENTRANCE WAY

NEW DOUBLE
DOORS
CENTRED ON
BATH TUB

SCALE 1:50

symmetrical line of the new room

▌ the remainder of the redundant entrance
was transformed into a **storage closet**
accessed from the hallway. It was therefore
not necessary to block up the old doorway,
only to hang a new door opening outwards

KEY

▇ BATHROOM		▇ HALL	
▇ BEDROOM		▇ SERVICE ACCESS	
▇ MASTER		▇ STORAGE	

When your room becomes your wall

ARCHITECT: JONATHAN CLARK

One of the assumptions that our activity-based perception of rooms often leads us to make is that kitchens must either be rooms in their own right, or well-defined sections of larger areas. On a limited footprint, creating these well-defined layouts can be wasteful of space.

Equally, bathrooms tend to be allocated some of the smallest spaces in our homes. Their arrangements are often driven either by ease of linking up to existing service outlets or by the logistics of using the bath, basin and toilet comfortably.

This apartment shows how, in a single property, a fully functioning kitchen can be lost against a wall and a tiny bathroom given a character and depth usually only found in far larger rooms.

Objectives

■ to install all the usual facilities of a high-specification kitchen but in the configuration that occupies the smallest possible footprint

■ to make an impressive feature of the kitchen once installed

■ to retain the relaxed feeling of the main living area

■ to remodel the bathroom and create a three-dimensional area of interest

■ to maximize storage space throughout the apartment

■ to maintain the two existing bedrooms in their present positions

ORIGINAL FLOOR PLAN

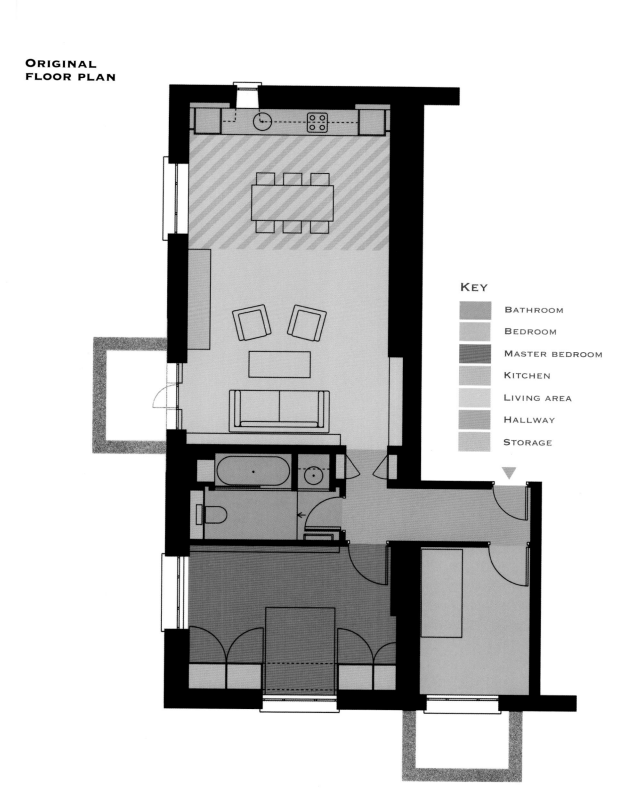

KEY

- BATHROOM
- BEDROOM
- MASTER BEDROOM
- KITCHEN
- LIVING AREA
- HALLWAY
- STORAGE

A kitchen wall to accommodate The configuration of this apartment sites the kitchen in a straight run against the far wall of the main living space. The shape is effectively the same as that found in any number of 'galley' kitchen layouts. But here a more impressive visual statement can be made.

While having the fridge, sink and oven/hob in a line is not ideal, the elements that make up this kitchen are no less than you would expect to find in any well-equipped kitchen, but it occupies a space of little more than 60cm across the end of the room.

Clever lighting defines the kitchen area and gives a certain separation.

FLOOR PLAN

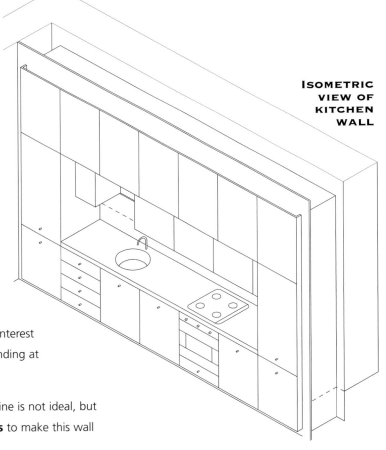

ISOMETRIC VIEW OF KITCHEN WALL

▪ the **kitchen** wall was designed around a small window in the wall, bringing both daylight and interest to the area – especially when standing at the sink

▪ fridge, sink and cooker/hob in a line is not ideal, but there are sufficient **worksurfaces** to make this wall kitchen practical for daily use

▪ clever lighting is essential to bring the area to life and give it definition apart from the **living/dining area**, while still blending it with the latter

A bathroom that defies the eye

The secret to creating a bathroom that works on a practical as well as an aesthetic level is to design spaces that blend seamlessly into each other, but that also define themselves individually.

This bathroom immediately deceives the eye as to its actual size. The cleverly lit platform to the bath and toilet area, and the fact that the bath and basin form divided modules – both are mood-lit – mean that the bathroom immediately feels much larger than it is because of the varying levels of depth, height and aspect.

- **two modules** line the bathroom: the divided basin/bath unit and the storage wall behind the toilet

- this **storage wall** also gives aesthetic and practical alcove storage for the bath area

- the **basin/bath unit** adds depth to the room while giving definition to the vanity and bathing areas

- the bath and toilet are on a **raised platform**, which adds a sense of height to the bathroom

- clever **lighting** washes the area with light and creates mood and character

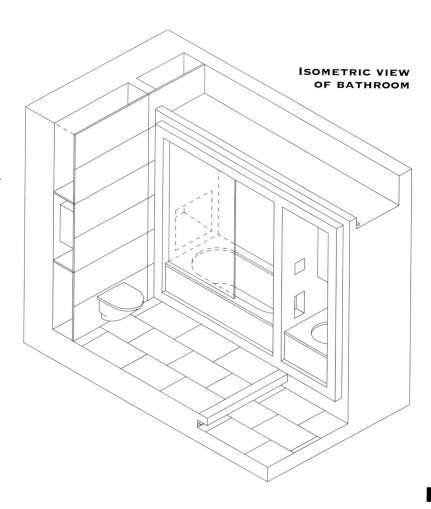

ISOMETRIC VIEW OF BATHROOM

Your own dream island kitchen

ARCHITECT: SPENCE HARRIS HOGAN

Creating a well-functioning kitchen within a large space can present as many challenges as being limited to a small space. In a large kitchen, it is essential to use all available space – but cleverly – so that getting from one working point to another does not feel like crossing a football pitch.

A large central island is critical to the configuration, especially in a kitchen as large as the one illustrated. This becomes the hub of activity with its extensive hob, single vegetable sink, double utility sinks, ample worksurfaces and breakfast bar at one end. Immediately to hand behind the hob are the double fridge freezer and double wall ovens.

Maximum circulation space is provided all around the central island, allowing passage to and from the large breakfast room, the garden and the living room, sited down steps to the left of the kitchen.

Objectives

■ to create a well-functioning kitchen within a large open-plan space

■ to ensure that circulation is not impeded from the adjacent rooms

■ to ensure that the kitchen is aesthetically pleasing, as it is open plan to the living room to its left

■ to provide white goods and state-of-the-art kitchen equipment within practical distances of each other

Solutions

■ a **central island** became the practical and aesthetic focal point of this kitchen

■ the island includes a **double utility sink**, a **single vegetable sink**, a **six-ring hob**, a large overhead **extractor hood**, and extensive worksurfaces with a **breakfast bar** at one end

■ a **double fridge freezer** caters to the needs of a large family and is sited conveniently behind the hob

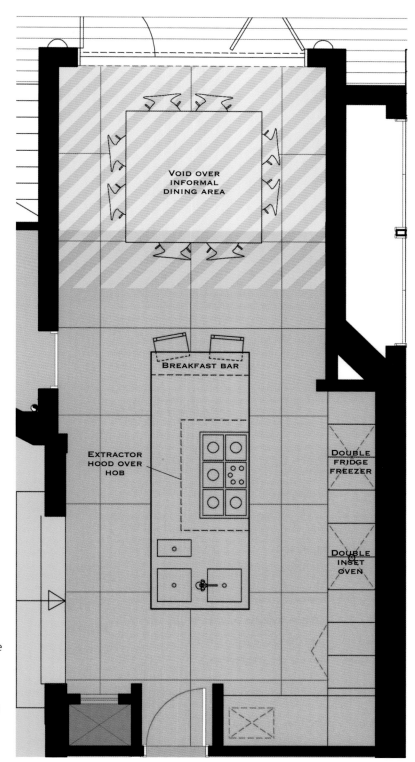

VOID OVER
INFORMAL
DINING AREA

BREAKFAST BAR

EXTRACTOR
HOOD OVER
HOB

DOUBLE
FRIDGE
FREEZER

DOUBLE
INSET
OVEN

KEY

DUMB WAITER

HALLWAY

KITCHEN

LIVING AREA

STORAGE

■ a **double wall oven** is also within easy reach of worksurfaces, sink and hob

■ extensive work elsewhere in the house at the time of fitting the kitchen enabled the installation of a **dumb waiter** which leads to the formal dining room and master suite above

SCALE 1:50

Folding away the dining room

DESIGNER: PAULA ROBINSON DESIGN GROUP

This newly converted city apartment was purchased as a pied-à-terre and had to undergo a number of changes to meet the client's requirements. During the week, it only needed to accommodate one person, but on some weekends an entire family of five could be in residence. In the main living area, the owner did not want space wasted on a dining table that could seat the whole family as it would have only occasional use. An innovative solution was called for that would be practical, space efficient and aesthetically pleasing.

A sofa bed was also required, but access to the flat was too tight through the narrow entrance hall to manoeuvre a sofa bed into the living room. A solution had to be found.

Objectives

■ to provide **dining space** for five people when the apartment was fully occupied

■ as it would only occasionally be fully occupied, the solution should **not include a large table,** which would dominate the space and limit the apartment's use for social gatherings

■ **aesthetics** should be a priority in any solution

■ to provide **overflow sleeping** facilities

■ to overcome the problem of the small entrance hall, which was too small to allow a conventional **sofa bed** to be manoeuvred through it

Solutions

■ in dining mode, a table – concealed behind a decorative shutter – pulls down from a recess in part of the false wall

■ the table's size was calculated to easily seat five

■ seating for the table is in the form of five padded, fabric covered cubes that, when not in use as

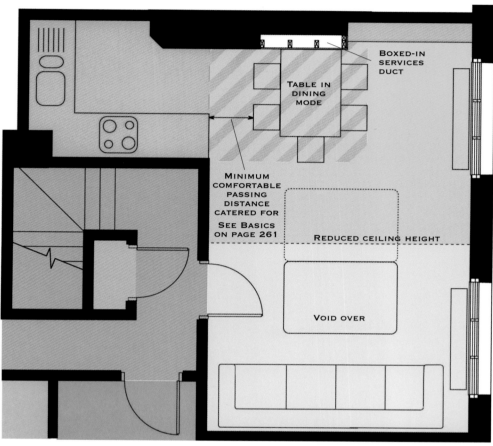

BOXED-IN
SERVICES
DUCT

TABLE IN
DINING
MODE

MINIMUM
COMFORTABLE
PASSING
DISTANCE
CATERED FOR
SEE BASICS
ON PAGE 261

REDUCED CEILING HEIGHT

VOID OVER

KEY

SCALE 1:50

BATHROOM   HALLWAY   LIVING AREA

BEDROOM   KITCHEN   STORAGE

dining stools, stack into an interesting sculptural
shape that blends into the room's design

■ in decorative mode, the table folds away out of
sight and only the shutter remains as part of the
living room's decoration

■ the tailor-made padded ottoman, designed to fit
through the entrance hall, opens out into a sofa
bed whenever additional sleeping space is required.
When not in bed use, it serves as a coffee
table/comfortable footrest

THE LENGTH OF A TABLE LIKE THIS, WHEN
FOLDED DOWN, WILL BE GOVERNED BY THE
HEIGHT OF THE CEILING, LESS 72CM – THE
STANDARD HEIGHT FROM THE FLOOR FOR A
DINING TABLE, SEE BASICS ON PAGE 260.

CONCEALING THE TABLE WAS POSSIBLE
BECAUSE OF A VOID BEHIND PLASTERBOARD
INSTALLED TO COVER AN UNEVEN SERVICES
DUCT. IF YOUR ROOM HAS SOLID WALLS,
YOU COULD CREATE YOUR OWN MOCK VOID
FOR THIS PURPOSE.

A few insights before you begin

*O*ne of the most important aspects of reconfiguring a property is the groundwork that you do beforehand. First steps include deciding which professionals to include and considering some of the issues you will be faced with.

Before launching into major works, be very clear in your own mind what your objectives are for the reconfiguration of your property. This will help you to come up with your own initial design concept and will greatly help you when it comes to briefing your suppliers.

The starting point for reconfiguring a space – when you have the luxury of a blank canvas – is to pay close attention to your lifestyle needs. A home requires a certain logic and order to it that will work for you. Ask yourself some searching questions. First, consider where you spend the majority of your time. Is it in the kitchen, the family room, the living room, the home office, the bedroom? Next, look at which activities are an essential part of your daily routine. Socializing, cooking, working at a computer, watching television: establish a priority order for these. Then, look at how children fit into the picture. Consider how well your home caters to their current ages and needs – and their future needs. Don't forget the animals and, finally, your guests: are they are a frequent pleasure, or a chore? Would a lack of guest accommodation deter them? Would segregating them as much as possible keep you sane?

Everybody's needs and requirements are different, and it is important that your home caters to your lifestyle and aspirations.

However, balancing personal lifestyle with resale value is important for most of us. The secret here is to avoid extremes. Don't be like the client who wanted to do away with the kitchen altogether because she never cooked. And don't be tempted to install only showers throughout your home if you dislike baths. You will alienate a large chunk of the resale market. At the same time, there is no point in painting all the walls 'neutral' magnolia and having sand-coloured carpets. This is your home you are dealing with, not simply an investment commodity, and you must be comfortable there. So finding the middle ground between your needs and the long term is the key.

Planning ahead with a good team

BUDGET, TIMING AND DISRUPTION

Once you have established your objectives, turn your attention to your budget, how you will cope with living on a building site and the date by which all work must be completed. All too often, the whole building scheme ends up costing more, taking longer and upsetting your day-to-day life more than you ever anticipated. Be realistic and prepare yourself for this.

Decide your absolute maximum spend on the project as a whole, and the date when all work really must be finished. Reduce both of these by a third and make these results

MOVING OUT

BUILDERS CAN WORK FAR MORE EFFICIENTLY IN AN EMPTY PROPERTY. THEY DON'T HAVE TO MAINTAIN A POWER SUPPLY AND THE WATER CAN BE TURNED OFF AT ANY TIME. THEY ALSO DON'T NEED TO CLEAN UP AT THE END OF EACH WORKING DAY.

THE COST OF MOVING OUT OF THE PREMISES DURING WORKS MAY BE OFFSET BY A REDUCTION IN THE TIME THE BUILDERS NEED TO BE ON SITE. BEAR THIS IN MIND WHEN CALCULATING COSTS.

known to whoever is co-ordinating the project at the outset – keeping the real figure and date strictly to yourself. This will leave you room for manoeuvre as things progress.

SAFEGUARD THE FINISHED PRODUCT

When the budget and timeline over-run – as a result of problems early on in a project – too often the only option left to the client is to skimp on the finishing touches. This can be disastrous. However superb the design and construction, it is not going to look impressive if complemented by aluminium door handles, basic light fittings and carpet tiles on the floor.

GET THE PROFESSIONALS INVOLVED

The chances of finding yourself in this situation can be minimized by seeking professional advice from the outset. Any perceived additional cost here should be more than compensated for by savings made on avoiding unnecessary problems or delays later in the project.

Much of what you pay for in terms of professional advice is the selection of a good-quality builder, appropriate for your particular project. Professionals will be better placed to recommend builders than will friends, neighbours or telephone directories.

For all but simple building jobs, you are likely to require input from an architect, a structural engineer, an interior designer and, of course, a builder.

Achieving a successful project

The cost of the design and supervision of quality building work can vary significantly. However, the more design and decision-making that is carried out pre-project, the better the project will be, and the more accurately you will be able to forecast costs.

GET EVERYONE INVOLVED AT ONCE

Try to involve as many of the suppliers as soon as possible in the planning stage. An architectural design prepared in isolation often leads to more expensive and difficult-to-build designs.

THE TRADES AND THEIR ROLES

THE ARCHITECT WILL:

- produce alternative plan and elevation design drawings for your approval
- prepare a planning application and apply for building regulations approval
- introduce other professional advisors as required
- obtain various quotations from known builders of suitable quality
- prepare a contract for the building works to safeguard payment and completion dates
- inspect progress of building work

THE STRUCTURAL ENGINEER WILL:

- prepare technical specifications (foundations, walls, beams, floors, roofs etc.)
- make formal calculations relating to the design plans to ensure that the resulting structure is safe to use
- carefully check any openings in, or removal of, walls in the property to ensure that the stability of the house is not compromised

THE INTERIOR DESIGNER WILL:

- add the heart and soul to the work in terms of colours, textures, fabrics, lighting, furniture layout and the positions of any necessary power and wiring outlets
- ensure that the whole scheme is styled to blend in with your existing surroundings

THE BUILDER WILL:

- carry out the actual work as defined by the drawings, calculations and design specifications drawn up by the previous three professionals

In reality, there may well be some crossover of abilities between these professionals, but remember they are from different disciplines. Each will concentrate on their own area of expertise, possibly at the expense of another.

Obtain early budget price checks to avoid abortive design costs and loss of valuable time.

THE IMPORTANCE OF RELEVANT PERMISSIONS

If you do decide, for whatever reason, not to involve professional advisors, do not be tempted to circumvent planning permission and building regulations. Irritating though some of the rules and regulations may be, they are there for your own protection, as well as that of your neighbours. If you decide to proceed without the official approval, you run the risk of getting caught out, particularly on re-sale, when a prospective purchaser's lawyer will want to see the relevant permissions.

There is a further point to remember if you are working within an apartment block, or a property that has communal space. It is essential to get your neighbours' approval – or, in the UK, the approval of the managing agent and freeholders – prior to carrying out any construction work. Moving the locations of kitchens and bathrooms in apartment blocks (UK and US) is rarely sanctioned, as all services tend to be built in a line.

EXTENSIONS

Planning issues will dictate the volume – in relation to the size of the original structure – that any extension can occupy, as well as the proximity to its boundaries. A terraced house can usually be extended only to the rear. A detached house offers the best opportunity to extend at the side of the property.

Construction considerations

REMOVING WALLS

Before planning a sweeping removal of internal walls in your home to create a vast open space, it is important to bear in mind the original structure of the building. Remember that the building will have been designed as a whole, with each of its elements giving strength to another – the sum total of its parts adding up to a stable unit. While building methods have changed over the years and variations exist between types of construction – blockwork and timber-frame detached buildings, brick-built terraces and steel-reinforced concrete multi-storey blocks – one adage generally holds true: if you take something away, you are likely to have to put something back in its place. Though exceptions exist, any division between two spaces will probably offer some degree of support, not only to the structural elements above it, but also to those on either side.

So how do you decide which walls you can and can't remove? Well, it's safe to assume that a thick, solid-sounding wall is going to cost more to open up or remove than a thin, hollow-sounding one. But only a structural engineer can give you a definitive answer to this question. It is important to seek this advice.

STEELWORK

Even a relatively simple extension can involve putting in a considerable amount of steelwork. However, this does allow for an almost seamless flow to be created between old and newly expanded or opened-up space, unfettered by archways or alcoves.

BASIC RULE

IF YOU TAKE SOMETHING AWAY, YOU ARE LIKELY TO HAVE TO PUT SOMETHING BACK IN ITS PLACE.

A THICK, SOLID-SOUNDING WALL IS GOING TO COST MORE TO OPEN UP OR REMOVE THAN A THIN, HOLLOW-SOUNDING ONE.

This minimalist feel can completely alter the character of the standard terraced house configuration. The walls of the upper floors can be supported almost entirely on a steel 'cage', albeit with the aid of strategically placed pillars.

As well as the steel beams – often referred to as RSJs, or rolled steel joists – that will be installed and concealed in walls and ceilings, sections may need to be laid beneath the floor on their own concrete bases before being bolted to the uprights and cross-members, completing the rigid cage. All this makes steelwork the favourite for enabling maximum reconfiguration of internal space.

CONCRETE LINTELS AND TIMBER

More modest support is offered by concrete lintels or thick timber sections. These would typically be used when making an opening in a wall rather than removing the wall completely.

THE KNOCK-ON EFFECT

Replacing support won't be the only issue you need to consider before attacking a wall. Remember that you will also have to deal with the floor, walls and ceiling in that area. Unless the floor was carpeted, it will be almost impossible to disguise a repair between the two opened-up areas. New flooring will be required on either side. Ceilings will need replastering. Electrical points and switches will need relocating from the lost wall. The rule then is: only move a wall if it will offer a significant benefit to the new layout. Further, there is no point in doing things by half measure – once you have disturbed an area, go for maximum reconfiguration to make the changes worthwile.

FLOORING

SEE BOX ON FLOORING ON PAGE 249

Basics for kitchens and bathrooms

KITCHENS

If you follow the basic triangle rule with kitchen design, you will never go far wrong. The fridge, sink and hob/oven must be positioned in a triangle in order to have a kitchen that functions well (see page 260). All three items must have sufficient work surfaces around them to make them functional. To have a hob, sink and fridge all immediately next to each other would be very impractical.

WORKTOPS TO CHOOSE FROM

Laminate worktop is the most common and cheapest surface. Laminate is made by coating compressed particle board in a layer of tough vinyl with a rounded front edge. It is available in many colours and patterns but is susceptible to scratching and scorching, and water getting into any joints will cause a problem.

Wood worktop is available in a variety of hardwoods. It gives a wonderfully warm feeling – both visually and to the touch. However, it requires some maintenance and is easily damaged by hot pans and knives. It will cost anything from two to four times the price of laminate.

Corian worktop is made up of a solid layer of plastic, cast to the layout of your cabinets and with the sink integrated into the moulding. It offers excellent hygiene standards – having no joints around the sink – and is very durable. It is similar in cost to stainless steel and granite.

Granite worktop is extremely durable and brings an opulent look to any kitchen, but be careful not to put your crystal glasses down on it too violently! It is available in a large variety of thicknesses and colours – and prices may vary greatly.

Stainless steel worktop is very stylish and contemporary to look at. It is also hygienic, practical and durable. As with Corian, sinks of various shapes and sizes – and often a splashback as well – can be incorporated in the same single piece of steel. This, coupled with various profiles formed into the front edge, guarantees a germ-free, long-lasting, low-maintenance surface that looks great.

Tadelakt worktop is a shiny, lime-based plaster historically used in Morocco. Tadelakt can be made water-resistant and reasonably hardwearing. While labour intensive to apply, it is ideal for bringing texture and interest to your kitchen. Despite being an old, traditional material, it can give a surprisingly contemporary and striking effect. Pigments can be added to key into a chosen colour scheme.

Never skimp on work surfaces: more is definitely better than less. If you have a large kitchen with a lot of space in the centre, consider a central island, a table or a butcher's block to make life easier.

BATHROOMS

A bathroom layout should not be reminiscent of something you would expect to find on a small boat. Cramped space is never good to live with, and can be a disaster for resale purposes.

Bathroom fittings – like kitchen fittings – need to be high-quality. Don't be tempted to skimp. Cheap fittings are unpleasant to live with, unhelpful for resale purposes and never value for money.

Test your chosen basin and taps together prior to purchase to ensure that they are in proportion and that the water from the spout will be easily accessible. This is particularly important if you are opting for surface-mounted basins, which sit on top of the vanity unit itself. If you opt for a wall-mounted spout for a dish-shaped basin, be sure the taps are positioned so that the spout will 'vent' close to the centre of the bowl. Otherwise, a strong jet of water may splash out of the opposite side.

WET ROOMS

Wet rooms are not cheap to install, even in small spaces. There are so many things to get right, and the list of things that can go wrong is lengthy. You need highly skilled professionals to carry out the project from start to finish.

USE A COMPETENT TILER

An excellent tiler is indispensable. He/she will need to get the look of your chosen tiles right. Remember that all your walls and floor will be tiled – a very large surface area that will easily show any errors of calculation on the tiler's behalf. And, beyond aesthetics, he/she will need to get the falls right, otherwise the water will not drain away properly and will sit in pools over the floor. This is both a nuisance and a hazard, as we all know how lethal wet tiled surfaces can be. Be sure, too, that your chosen tiles have a non-slip surface.

WATER SEEPAGE AND 'TANKING'

Be certain that your contractor plans to deal with water seepage and 'tanking' appropriately. The grout between tiles can't be guaranteed to prevent water seeping through, and the joints between level and vertical surfaces are particularly vulnerable to leaks. These latter joints must always be sealed with a suitable flexible silicon sealant.

Capillary action can carry any water that does seep through the grout sideways and upwards, so the floor and walls must be 'tanked': a waterproof membrane is laid beneath the tiles to cover the entire floor and return up the walls to form a 'pond'. The only outlet for water is into the special wet area drain unit in the wet area floor – below the surface of the tiles. If your budget will allow, and the area is not too large, a stainless steel tray below the tiles is a safer solution.

GET ONE CONTRACTOR TO CARRY OUT THE INSTALLATION OF THE ENTIRE WET ROOM. THAT WAY, NOT ONLY DO YOU HAVE ONE POINT OF CONTACT FOR ANY COMPLAINTS BUT ALSO EACH ASPECT OF THE WORK SHOULD BE CARRIED OUT WITH DUE REGARD FOR EVERY OTHER.

VERTICAL AND HORIZONTAL JOINTS SHOULD ALWAYS BE SEALED WITH A FLEXIBLE SILICON SEALANT.

KEEPING IT WARM AND DRY UNDERFOOT

If you are planning to have underfloor heating, it is absolutely essential that this is installed by professionals – and this need not be outrageous in cost.

Once the tiles are laid, major disruption and cost will be incurred if any services need to be accessed under the floor. Be sure your contractor checks that pipework and electrical circuits are sound and will not need any maintenance.

FLOORING OPTIONS

Twist-pile carpets are less expensive than velvet pile and are generally very hardwearing. Their drawbacks are their look and feel (they can appear cheap), and the limited range of colours.

Velvet pile carpets come in any number of colours, thicknesses and prices. Investing in a good-quality carpet with high wool content is always advisable. Cleaned annually, a quality carpet will have years of wear in it.

Wood flooring ranges from the expensive but durable solid wood floor, to plankwood, to the cheaper but less resilient veneered wood and, finally, the grand-daddy of character, the reclaimed wood floor. Invest in quality and you will not be disappointed in the long term. A solid wood floor can be sanded and resealed when it becomes worn, scratched and stained. In contrast, a veneered wood floor cannot. Once it has become worn and marked, the only option is to replace it. Be sure to use a good fitter. the sublime effect of a wood floor can be ruined if it is not properly installed.

Natural stone, concrete, metal, ceramic, textural resin-based, glass, rubber and even **leather** floors can be exotic, unusual and tempting! Think colour, texture, pattern and imagination, and you're on the wavelength of these floors.

Marble, travertine, limestone, sandstone and **slate** are common types of natural stone flooring.

Three finishes are generally available:

- Riven: rough and irregular. Fantastic in kitchens or bathrooms, but not easy to keep clean
- Honed: ground to a smooth matt sheen
- Polished: a smart high-gloss surface, but it will become scratched in a short space of time

While the materials themselves can be expensive, the preparation of the sub-floor and the laying of the flooring itself can be very costly. Maintenance is also a major issue to bear in mind: natural stone will always look better than tiles, but, once laid, tiles can be forgotten.

Lighting basics

A frequent problem in apartment buildings – especially in the US – is bathrooms and kitchens that lack a window. While ventilation is obviously dealt with by extractor fans, clever lighting solutions can sometimes be the only way to combat the feeling of being trapped in a box.

GO MOODY IN THE KITCHEN ...

Once you have taken care of the all-important central lighting to flood the kitchen or bathroom with maximum light whenever required, consider some moody options to make areas seem to float between the floor and ceiling.

In a kitchen, conceal strip lights between the bottom of the base cabinets and the skirting/base board. This will give an eerie, continuous line of light between the base cabinets and the floor, making the cabinets appear to float above the floor. Install strip lights on top of the cabinets to make the top cabinets appear to float in the same way.

Don't forget the standard under-cabinet lighting, which is fitted underneath the top cabinets to throw light on the worksurface below.

... AND MOODY IN THE BATHROOM

The same principle applies to the bathroom. Get your bath to 'float' too by installing a line of concealed strip lights at the base of your bath panel. But for safety reasons in the UK, be absolutely sure that you are using sealed bathroom fittings – no bare bulbs please!

WHEN BUYING LIGHTS FOR A BATHROOM, ALWAYS CHECK WITH YOUR SUPPLIER THEY CONFORM TO THE CORRECT IP RATING FOR THE POSITION IN WHICH THEY WILL BE FITTED.

OPAQUE GLASS PANELS

Backlit, opaque or acid-etched glass panels can add to the illusion of extra light and space. Done well, they can mimic an opaque glazed window and thus help to minimise the feeling of claustrophobia in a small, dark space without natural daylight.

LIGHTING PELMETS

An architectural feature and an indirect source of light to consider is a lighting pelmet. This runs around a room at cornice height, opening upwards, with the purpose of throwing light onto the ceiling.

SKIRTING LIGHTING

Skirting lights give a stunning visual effect and have many different applications. They are obviously very practical on stairs, as they give clear definition to treads and risers – no more stumbling! In a corridor, they make a great night light, as the light they cast is less obtrusive than that of ceiling fittings.

Skirting lights also look spectacular installed as uplighters in the floors of any room – parallel to the walls. Instead of being directed horizontally at skirting height, they can then be positioned to highlight artwork on the walls in a minimalist decor.

Remember that the glass covers of skirting and floor lights will get hot – not sufficiently hot to burn or blister skin – but not enough to alarm a small child. LED versions –

WASHING THE CEILING WITH LIGHT LOOKS STRIKING, BUT THIS WILL HIGHLIGHT EVERY MINUTE CRACK AND IMPERFECTION. YOU MAY NEED TO RE-SKIM THE ENTIRE SURFACE.

MIRRORS WORK

DON'T BE AFRAID TO USE FLOOR-TO-CEILING MIRRORS ON KITCHEN WALLS TO MAXIMIZE THE SENSE OF SPACE. IT WORKS IN THE BATHROOM, SO DON'T HESITATE TO USE THE SAME TRICK IN THE KITCHEN.

which don't get nearly as hot – are available in most styles, though they will not be as bright.

You have two choices when positioning skirting lights: as close as possible to the floor so that they cast a pencil of light across the floor, or higher up so that they create a small pool of light on the opposite wall, which will then bounce back as a softer, diffused localized area of light.

GLASS WALLS

WHY CHOOSE A GLASS WALL?

Glass walls between rooms are wonderful for maximizing available daylight. They also give an optical illusion of space and are very contemporary in feel. They are particularly good options when soundproofing is an issue, as glass, particularly at the widths required for room dividers – 12mm or more – is surprisingly good for muffling sound.

A QUESTION OF PRIVACY

Privacy between the two rooms divided by a glass wall can be achieved in a number of ways. The most striking – but pricey – option is Privalite glass, which goes from clear to opaque at the touch of a button.

A cost-effective solution if you want light transmission and privacy is muslin curtains fitted on a discreet ceiling-mounted track. Alternatively, self-lined curtains will block light transmission, but will give complete privacy.

HEATED GLASS

Glass can now even replace radiators, generating

heat at the flick of a switch. 'Glasstherm' has a heating element invisibly integrated into the glass. It can be installed in addition to the Privalite system, giving warmth and privacy in one.

Glasstherm can be used between rooms, but is also ideal for conservatories.

GLASS BLOCK WALLS

If the prospect of an entire wall of glass is too much – or too costly – consider the more cost-effective option of glass block walls. These are ideal for dark stairways, corridors, small areas that lack daylight and rooms that currently receive no natural light at all.

Glass block walls can either be made up entirely of glass blocks or, alternatively, concrete blocks can be used to form the main structure, with glass blocks interspersed in whatever configuration you choose. This gives a very contemporary look, although less light will be made available to a dark area.

If the wall forms part of an escape corridor, the glass blocks will need to be fire-resistant.

Colour
basics

MAKING SPACES FLOW, NOT JAR

Adding character to a property by deploying a colour palette requires skill and a lot of thought. Rooms and areas need to give the impression of flowing into one another. At no point should you walk from one space into another and be jarred by the contrast.

Changes in colour should be subtle and pleasing, something that you are gradually aware of, not suddenly hit by. If each room is painted a distinct colour, you can end up with a home that feels like a series of multicoloured boxes stuck together – a Rubik's Cube is not your goal.

A SPLASH OF STRONG COLOUR INSTEAD

If you're still undeterred and you just can't resist a wild colour moment, try to restrict yourself to the odd splash of colour. The now popular technique of painting one wall in a strong contrasting colour is very effective in contemporary homes, as it adds both an architectural feel and a sense that some thought and attention have gone into the space.

Choosing the right wall to have the contrast colour treatment – and the right colour to apply – is very important. The colour of the contrast wall needs to add dimension to the room without leaping out at you or being too oppressive. You really do need to have a flair for colour to get this right. If in doubt, get an expert opinion.

TEST THE THEORY FIRST

Always paint a sample section of wall to test the colour before purchasing several litres of paint. Don't rely on paint charts for accuracy in choosing your colour. These small swatches of colour can look completely different painted onto a whole expanse of wall. Colour looks different according to light levels, other surrounding colours, and the angle of the wall it is painted on.

DARK COLOURS DISGUISE SMALL SPACES

Dark colours help to confuse the eye as to the exact dimensions of a space. For a narrow corridor with a high ceiling, a dark colour – especially black – will disguise the less than ideal proportions. A lighter colour will only accentuate them.

BOLD COLOUR FOR HALLWAYS

Use colour boldly in areas that you don't spend extended amounts of time in, such as hallways, utility rooms, etc. Be more cautious with your colour choices in areas that are in constant daily use. Pay particular attention to bedroom colour: this sets your mood for the rest of the day when you wake up.

SEE ALSO BOX ON COLOUR ON PAGES 142–3.

Door basics

FOR TIGHT SPACES TRY SPLIT DOORS ...

When space is tight (especially in bathrooms and kitchens), consider an alternative to a single door opening into the space. A single door width can be split into two small double doors. This solution works no matter what style of door you are installing – even swing doors in the US.

... OR SLIDING DOORS

An alternative to double doors for small spaces is sliding doors – especially for a sleek, contemporary interior. Do be sure that the doors are high-quality, as there is nothing worse than cheap sliding doors with mechanisms that scrape and rumble as the door is moved.

QUALITY AND BLENDING WITH THE ROOM

Doors must be solid in weight and feel. Light, thin doors give a property a 'cheap' feeling. Doors must not contrast too strongly with the rest of a small room. Installing dark wood doors with white-, cream- or light-coloured walls can be a disaster in a small space.

CLOSET DOORS – AN OPAQUE STATEMENT

Try fitting doors that include opaque glass. The best way to achieve this glazed look is with simple door frames that hold single sheets of toughened glass. The single sheets will give a fine contemporary feel to the doors and room itself.

GETTING THE LOOK RIGHT

The glass can be sandblasted, or a cheaper option is to use an opaque film on clear glass. Inside the closets, try including concealed lighting strips (switched externally) to give a wash of light to the glass. This then becomes another source of mood lighting for the room.

If your property is more traditional in feel, consider installing closet doors with multiple panes of sandblasted glass instead of the more modern single pane.

Furniture basics

GETTING YOUR PROPORTIONS RIGHT

Your sense of proportions is vital in choosing furniture for rooms. You need to be able to visualize how each piece will look in situ. Instinctive answers are required for questions such as, 'Will this sofa dwarf the space or will it look ridiculously small?'

If in doubt, draw a floorplan of the room to scale – using the graph paper at the end of this chapter – measure the furniture pieces and then draw them in to scale. This will give you a good idea of whether furniture will work or not within a given space.

GETTING PAST THE FRONT DOOR

Be absolutely certain that your chosen sofa – or any large piece of furniture – can actually be manoeuvred into the property. Tight corridors and small windows are often a

---

METRIC & IMPERIAL MEASUREMENTS

Throughout this book, rather than giving two figures, we have chosen to use metric measurements only. For those more used to working in feet and inches, here is a ready reckoner – shown to one decimal place or the nearest eighth of an inch – to help convert to imperial units.

Inch	cm	Inch	cm	Feet	m	Feet	m
1	– 2.5	12	– 30.5	1	– 0.3	9'10"	– 3.0
2	– 5.1	15¾	– 40.0	2	– 0.6	10	– 3.1
3	– 7.6	18	– 45.7	3	– 0.9	11	– 3.4
4	– 10.2	19¾	– 50.0	3'3"	– 1.0	12	– 3.7
5	– 12.7	23⅝	– 60.0	4	– 1.2	13	– 4.0
6	– 15.2	24	– 61.0	5	– 1.5	13'2"	– 4.0
7	– 17.8	27½	– 70.0	6	– 1.8	14	– 4.3
8	– 20.3	31½	– 80.0	6'7"	– 2.0	15	– 4.6
9	– 22.9	35⅜	– 90.0	7	– 2.1	16	– 4.9
10	– 25.4	36	– 91.4	8	– 2.4	16'5"	– 5.0
11	– 27.9	39⅜	– 1.0m	9	– 2.7	20	– 6.1

$1ft^2 = 0.093m^2$ $1m^2 = 10.9ft^2$

problem, especially in new-build apartments. Measure the means of access (all doorways or any window) that the piece has to pass through.

Curtain basics

PATTERNED FABRICS

If your main objective is to make your property appear as light and spacious as possible, be cautious when it comes to pattern in curtain fabrics. Pattern does two things: first it draws the eye, then it creates an emotive response.

Remember that if you want to draw the gaze out and beyond the windows, you will not want the eye to be hijacked by loud, busy curtains. When the eye is distracted from looking out and beyond, a subconscious feeling of claustrophobia can be created.

KEEPING IT PLAIN AND SIMPLE

Plain and understated materials are the best choice for several reasons:

- They do not draw unnecessary attention to themselves, and thereby make a property appear less cramped.
- They will not make anybody's toes curl!
- They are always more cost-effective. A plain fabric can look stylish, elegant and expensive even if it was purchased at a bargain price.

But do remember to check that any fabric you choose meets all legal requirements on fire rating. Not all fabrics are flame-retardant, so do ask before purchasing.

Minimum measurement basics When planning a new layout on paper, you may find it difficult to visualize the actual space taken up by its various elements. This may lead to some convenient solutions on your plan turning out to be unfortunate mistakes in reality.

As a guide, here are some minimum comfortable distances and dimensions, broken down by room types, to take into account when planning your home.

Some common sizes and standard heights have also been included in each section.

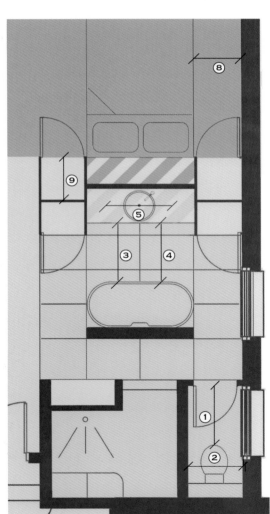

BATHROOMS

① minimum distance between a toilet bowl and a facing wall or door: **60cm**

② minimum comfortable width for a toilet: **60cm**

③ minimum 'drying off' distance between a bath or shower and a facing wall (or other obstruction): **70cm**

④ minimum bending space behind a basin: **70cm**

⑤ minimum elbow space to either side of a basin: **85cm**

⑥ minimum room dimensions needed to create a bathroom, based on these comfortable working distances: **2.3 x 1.6m** or **2.55 x 1.45m**

⑦ minimum room dimensions needed to create a shower room, based on these comfortable working distances: **1.65 x 1.4m**

COMMON BATH SIZES

Fitted baths: **170 x 75cm**. Also in various combinations between **150-170 x 75cm**, and **170-180 x 80cm**
Free-standing baths: from **140 x 70 cm** to **180 x 90cm**

BEDROOMS

⑧ minimum comfortable distance between a bed and a wall: **65cm**

⑨ minimum depth for internal measurement of a clothes-hanging closet: **50cm**

⑩ space needed for an adult to bend and reach into the base of a closet: **90cm**

⑪ space needed for an adult to kneel and open a bottom drawer: **1.2m**

⑫ minimum dimensions needed to create a double bedroom, based on these comfortable working distances: **2.65 x 2.65m**

COMMON BED SIZES

Single: **190 x 90cm**

Double: **190 x 135cm**

Queen size: **200 x 150cm** (also called King)

King size: **200 x 180cm** (also called Super King's size)

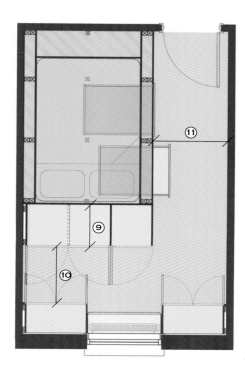

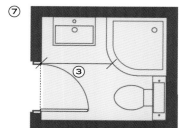

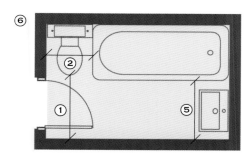

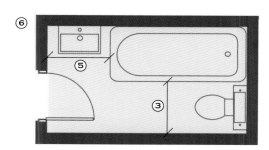

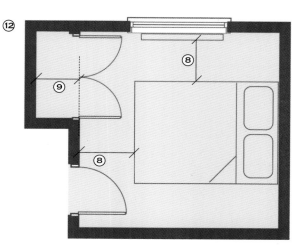

KITCHENs

① worktop overhang for feet to fit comfortably under a breakfast bar: **25cm**

② standard work top depth: **60cm**

③ standard appliance depth: **circa 57cm** (options up to **80cm**)

④ standard appliance width: **59.5cm** (options up to **90cm**)

⑤ standard main entrance door dimensions: **76 or 84 x 203cm**

⑥ standard interior door dimensions: **61, 69 or 74 x 198cm**

⑦ kitchen 'working triangle' of fridge, cooker and sink: see page 246

Standard worktop height: **90cm**

Common table height – to underside of top: **72cm**

Common dining chair height – to top of seat: **45cm**

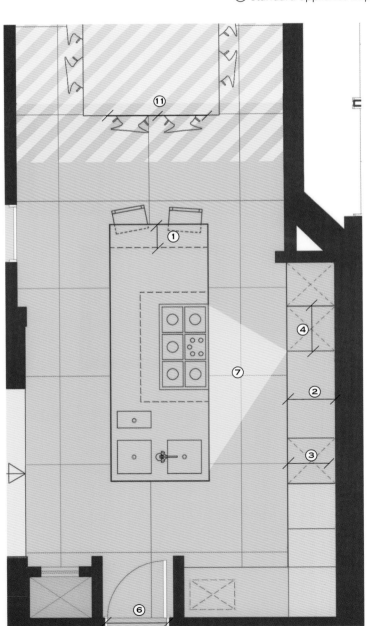

LIVING AREA

⑧ minumim passing distance behind a piece of furniture: **50cm**

⑨ minimum leg room between a sofa and a coffee table: **30cm**

⑩ minimum distance between a table and a wall to allow getting in and out of a chair: **70cm**

⑪ minimum comfortable space between diners at a table to allow for elbow room: **60cm**

⑫ minimum corridor width: **90cm**

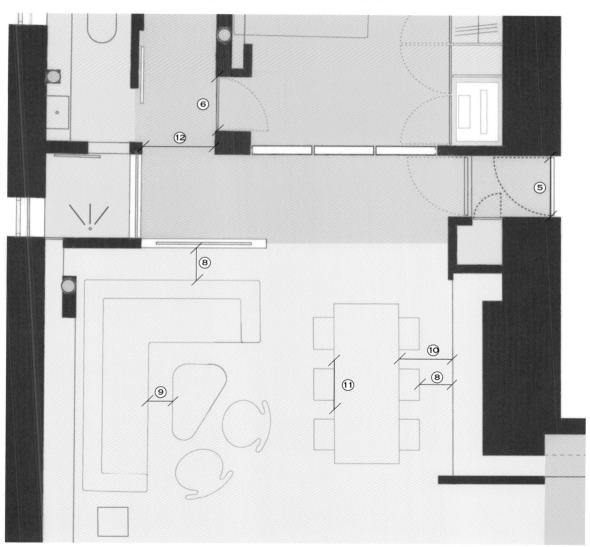

CONCLUSION

*Some final thoughts
on the homes of the future*

*S*ince cave-dwelling days, 'home' has taken on many façades and assumed many guises for all of us. But fundamentally, it has retained its age-old purpose of haven. Basically, home represents somewhere safe and warm for us to rest and recover. And in our current age of super-achievement, we need our safe havens more than ever!

Homes were once designed as showpieces for entertaining and impressing visitors, but today they are conceived first and foremost for the occupants – individuals who, for the most part, have less time and inclination to entertain. Where previous generations wanted to 'keep up appearances', a more *laissez faire* attitude has crept into our homes in this century. 'Take us as you find us' is now our creed.

Privacy is a passion of our modern, affluent society. Whereas people once clustered together for warmth and security, we now crave space and isolation.

Technology has taken care of most of our needs, from climate control to security and entertainment. It has given us a sense of power and control, but it has also bred a deep-rooted unhappiness in many people. Everyone tries to escape from sensory overload but, sadly, when we reach the sanctuary of our homes, we too often find that privacy is tantamount to isolation.

Homes speak eloquently of their owners as soon as you walk through the door: chaotic or spotless, filled with a lifetime's treasures or monastic in their simplicity. Today's homes are perfect illustrations of our busy lives. Many homes give the air of patiently waiting their turn in terms of where they fit into our priorities. Altered family structures and the fact that more and more people are living alone have meant that we have less time and energy to focus on our homes – despite our fascination with makeover shows and DIY.

Our thinking and our needs have transformed our lifestyles and our surroundings need to evolve to keep pace. Design has often taken inspiration from the past, but in order to adapt to contemporary living, we need to discover a new source of inspiration to meet our changing needs.

Looking for new inspiration

For centuries, our homes have referred back to the ideal of Greek and Roman architecture and the dictates of monument architecture. But, as the 21st century moves on, our need for a welcoming haven will grow ever stronger. Stark monuments will no longer work for us, and we will begin to understand that monument architecture does not provide us with any sense of shelter from the information age that we live in.

So where do we begin to look for new inspiration? Many believe that a wonderful starting point would be the architecture of nomadic cultures – otherwise known as portable architecture. This offers a very different perspective on domestic architecture and design, and is worth spending a little time exploring as we assess how to reconfigure and redefine our homes.

MONUMENT VERSUS PORTABLE ARCHITECTURE

To begin, let's take a brief look at some of the many
contrasts between our old, tried and trusted monument
architecture and the (to us) relatively unknown portable
architecture.

In the West, our sedentary lifestyles are contained within
homes that have, until recently, focused primarily on the
predominantly male concern with monument, façade and
permanence. Throughout Western history, men have been
the designers, builders, maintainers and owners of the
structures we live in. By contrast, in nomadic cultures
throughout the world, it is the women who create,
construct, dismantle and transport the home environment.
They also own the structure and its contents.

In the West, we are always in control of the environment in
which we live. To this day, members of nomadic cultures
live in harmony with the environment. From the
Mongolian yurt, to the Lapp kota, from the Sudanese
hadendowa to the south-west Moroccan tekna and the
North American tipi, nomadic dwellings provide focus and
stability for their inhabitants, despite the uncertainty of
nature with which they must live. In nomadic homes the
layout of the interior spaces remains identical each time the
inhabitants move camp. The position of the hearth, the altar
and the beds and the appointed spaces for family members
and guests are all fixed according to cultural dictates. This,

then, is the stability of these dwellings, whereas Western homes remain fixed in structure and façade only.

While the interior space of the nomadic tent has a highly structured organization, it is not based on rationalizing objects and their uses within the space. Instead, it is based on the very female dictate of interpersonal relationships and social sensitivity. Despite the physical confines of the space, there is cohesion, a sense that it does work as a whole. The space is organized around human need, not objects and appearance. The nomadic tent interior is crafted emotively, not logically. It is rich in colour, pattern, texture and symbolism. It is soft and malleable, created from minimally modified natural materials.

WORKING FROM THE INSIDE OUT

In portable architecture, a nurturing interior space is created in the face of an ever-threatening outside world. The constant assembling and dismantling of the tent is a form of creative expression: it is a collaborative creation, from the hands and hearts of women. It begins from the interior space and works progressively outwards to the exterior – in complete contrast to the design of Western architecture, which starts from the façade and works inwards.

This fundamental male/female difference in approaching space creation has also been demonstrated in Western psychological research. When young children play and create spatial configurations in play, the girls always emphasize inner space, while the boys usually emphasize external space.

LOOKING TO THE EAST

Let's now look to the culture and beliefs of the East, and feng shui. Here, we are reminded yet again that Western culture is very much alone in its homage to the dictates of monument architecture.

In China, there has always been an appreciation for the need of both yin (feminine) and yang (masculine) energy to balance life on all levels. The flow of chi (energy) in the home is considered vital to the health, happiness and wealth of the occupants.

As with portable architecture, the interior space in feng shui is highly organized, based on dictates that are anything but logical and appearance-driven. Again, interpersonal relationship, symbolism and colour come into play. Many Westerners have dismissed the Chinese art of placement as hocus pocus, but have been surprised to find that it actually does work.

The inspiration for our future homes Is our conclusion to be that in the future our homes may make a dramatic break from the past and instead be increasingly inspired by nomadic women's architecture or the cultures of the East? The possibility is intriguing. The reasoning behind this hypothesis has nothing to do with the feminist movement, but everything to do with a deeper understanding of human nature and its combined survival/nurture drive.

Obviously, our 21st century havens will never fully emulate the layout or lifestyle of nomadic cultures. But just imagine our homes evolving to become more in tune with our emotive and spiritual needs – an encouraging thought to say the very least.

We have come to understand that technology and communication represent a monument to masculine logic and order, but we find it impossible to live fulfilled lives if our homes follow the same dictates.

The concept of industrial practicality and durability giving way to sensory sensitivity in both the layout and contents of our homes would make for a refreshing change. Sight, sound, smell and touch would become primary considerations, with an emphasis on movement and change to keep the mind stimulated and alert.

We insist on nurturing our growing children with knowledge and experiences. As our new era encourages us to become more in tune with our own inner needs, we will become increasingly aware that our thirst for knowledge and novelty does not leave us in childhood; it is with us throughout our lives.

A home can be a true haven to us when it not only nurtures and protects us, but also stimulates and inspires us for the long term. It needs to take account of who we are and where we are headed. It needs to adapt to us – we do not need to adapt to it.

Planning our homes is all about planning our lives and where we would like them to lead us.

ACKNOWLEDGMENTS

Our sincere thanks and appreciation go to:

Carey Smith, our publisher, whose brain child *The Room Planner* was;
the **talented** and **innovative architects** who have contributed to this book;
Phillip Price, our architect;
Simon Pole, our structural engineer;
Sarah Lavelle, our editor, for all her hard work and sunny nature
throughout the project;
Margaret Gilbey and **Ali Glenny** for editing the text;
Rob Shreeve, our agent, for all his support and involvement throughout;
Sue Wilson for meticulous research; and
Leon Rossouw for support beyond the call of duty.

Paula's special thanks go to Phil for his endless attention to detail and his
superb work on the graphics and the design of this book.

CONTRIBUTORS

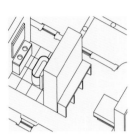

Hugh Broughton Architects

4 Addison Bridge Place

London W14 8XP

Telephone: + 44 (0) 20 7602 8840

Website: www.hbarchitects.co.uk

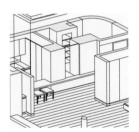

Jonathan Clark Architects

Second Floor,

34–35 Great Sutton Street,

London EC1V 0DX

Telephone: +44 (0) 20 7608 1111

Website: www.jonathanclarkarchitects.co.uk

Paula Robinson Design Group

22 Church Street

Winsham, Chard

Somerset TA20 4JD

Telephone: + 44 (0) 1460 30036

Website: www.paula-robinson.com

Rosemont Architecture

129 Putney Bridge Road

London SW15 2PA

Telephone: +44 (0) 20 8870 8622

E-mail: david@rosemont.co.uk

Spence Harris Hogan

1 Vencourt Place

Ravenscourt Park

London W6 9NU

Telephone: +44 (0) 20 8600 4171

Website: www.shh.co.uk

UV Architects

16–25 Underwood Street

London, N1 7JQ

Telephone: + 44 (0) 20 7490 3387

Website: www.uvarchitects.co.uk

USEFUL ADDRESSES

ARCHITECTURAL SALVAGE

Boiseries:
www.boiseries-deco.fr
+33 (0) 1 43 71 76 30

Lassco
www.lassco.co.uk
+44 (0) 20 7749 9944

Portes Anciennes:
www.portesanciennes.com
+33 (0) 4 90 92 13 13

Salvo
www.salvo.co.uk

BATHROOMS

CP Hart
www.cphart.co.uk
+44 (0) 20 7928 5866

CARPETS

Carpet Library
+44 (0) 20 7736 3664

CORNICE

The Classic Cornice Company
www.classiccornice.co.uk
+44 (0) 20 8874 0221

DOORS

The London Door Company
www.londondoor.co.uk
+44 (0) 20 7801 0877

FURNITURE RESTORATION

Twickenham Antiques
www.twickenhamantiques.com
+44 (0) 20 8894 5555

GLASS

Greenberg Glass Group
www.greenbergglass.co.uk
+44 (0) 151 207 2574

Luxcrete
www.luxcrete.co.uk
+44 (0) 20 8965 7292

Pilkington Glass
www.pilkington.com
+44 (0) 1744 692000

Preedy Glass
www.preedyglass.com
+44 (0) 20 7700 03770

Rankins (Glass) Company
www.rankinsglass.com
+44 (0) 20 7729 4200

HOME ORGANIZATION

Bebie Waller
www.simplyorganised.co.uk
07950 579 595

Your Concierge
www.yourconcierge.co.uk
+44 (0) 8700 761 961

HOME OFFICE

Lamb Macintosh
www.lambmacintosh.com
+44 (0) 1753 522369

LIGHTING

Absolute Action Ltd
www.absolute-action.com
+44 (0) 20 8874 7477

John Cullen Lighting
www.johncullenlighting.co.uk
+44 (0) 20 7371 5400

Lighting Direct
www.lighting-direct.co.uk
+44 (0) 1923 333100

Mr Resistor
www.mr-resistor.co.uk
+44 (0) 20 8874 2234

SKK
www.skk.net
+44 (0) 20 7434 4095

LIGHTING RESTORATION & REPAIR

Christopher Wray Lighting
www.christopher-wray.com
+44 (0) 20 7836 6869

Olympic Electronics
www.olympicelectronicsken.co.uk +44 (0) 20 7229 8983

LIGHT SWITCHES & FITTINGS

Forbes & Lomax
www.forbesandlomax.co.uk
+44 (0) 20 7738 0202

Siro DIY Uk Ltd
www.siro-diy.co.uk
+44 (0) 1827 51815

NATURAL STONE

Hard Rock Flooring
www.hardrockflooring.co.uk
+44 (0) 1296 658 755

Paris Ceramics
www.parisceramics.com
+44 (0) 20 7371 7778

Reed Harris
www.reedharris.co.uk
+44 (0) 20 7736 7511

PAINT (SPECIALIST)

Fired Earth
www.firedearth.co.uk
+44 (0) 1295 812315

JW Bollom & Company
www.bollom.com
+44 (0) 20 8658 2299

Paint Library
www.paintlibrary.co.uk
+44 (0) 20 7823 7755

Paint Services
www.paintservices.com
+44 (0) 1428 651246

Tor Coatings
www.ecplc.com
+44 (0) 161 480 3891

SOFAS (BESPOKE) & UPHOLSTERY

David Seyfried
www.davidseyfried.com
+44 (0) 20 7823 3848

Chance Chair Company
phillipa.eastaugh@btinternet.com
+44 (0) 20 8874 6249

SPECIALIST PAINT EFFECTS

Tim Saladin and **Roger Byrne**
+44 (0) 20 7385 1887

TILES

Fired Earth
www.firedearth.co.uk
+44 (0) 1295 814315

Paris Ceramics
www.parisceramics.com
+1 (212) 644 2728

Topps Tiles
www.toppstiles.co.uk
+44 (0) 800 783 6262

Worlds End Tiles
www.worldsendtiles.co.uk
+44 (0) 20 7819 2110

WORKTOPS (ALTERNATIVE MATERIALS)

Construction Resources
www.constructionresources.com
+44 (0) 20 7450 2211

GEC Anderson
www.gecanderson.co.uk
+44 (0) 1442 826 999
for stainless steel

Mass Surfaces
www.masssurfaces.co.uk
+44 (0) 870 241 8171
for concrete

Tierrafino
www.tierrafino.nl
+31 (0) 20 689 25 15
for tadelakt

STRUCTURAL ENGINEERS

Pole Associates
www.pole.co.uk
+44 (0) 20 8944 9955

TRADE AND PROFESSIONAL ASSOCIATIONS

Federation of Master Builders
www.fmb.org.uk
+44 (0) 20 7242 7583

Glass and Glazing Federation
www.ggf.org.uk
for local suppliers

Guild of Master Craftsmen
www.thegmcgroup.com
+44 (0) 1273 478 449

Institute of Plumbing
www.iphe.org.uk
+44 (0) 1708 472 791

Institute of Structural Engineers
www.istructe.org.uk
+44 (0) 20 7235 4535

NHBC (National House Building Council)
www.nhbc.co.uk
+44 (0) 1494 735363

NICEIC (National Inspection Council for Electrical Installation Contracting)
www.niceic.org.uk
+44 (0) 800 013 0431

Royal Institute of British Architects
www.riba.org
+44 (0) 20 7580 5533

Royal Institution of Chartered Surveyors
www.rics.org
+44 (0) 870 333 1600

INDEX

NOTES

YOUR PLANS SCALE 1:100

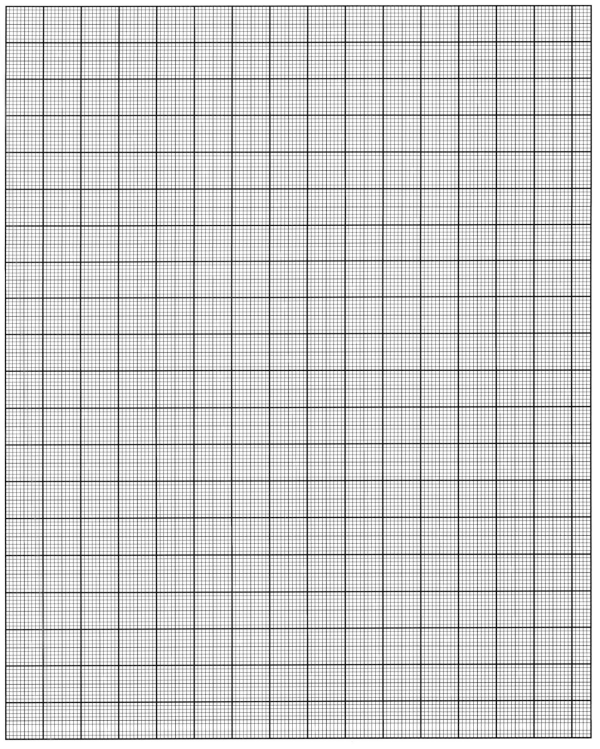

EACH LARGE SQUARE = 1M, EACH SMALL SQUARE = 10CM

NOTES

YOUR PLANS SCALE 1:100

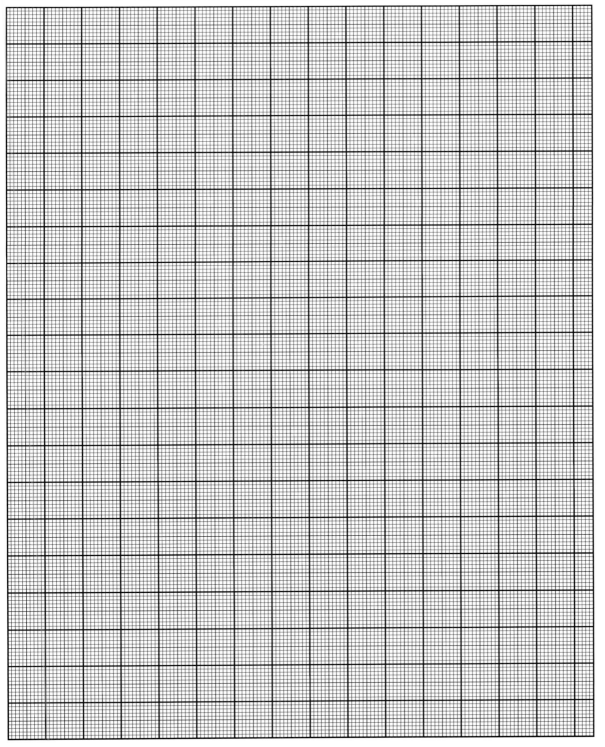

EACH LARGE SQUARE = 1M, EACH SMALL SQUARE = 10CM

NOTES

YOUR PLANS SCALE 1:50

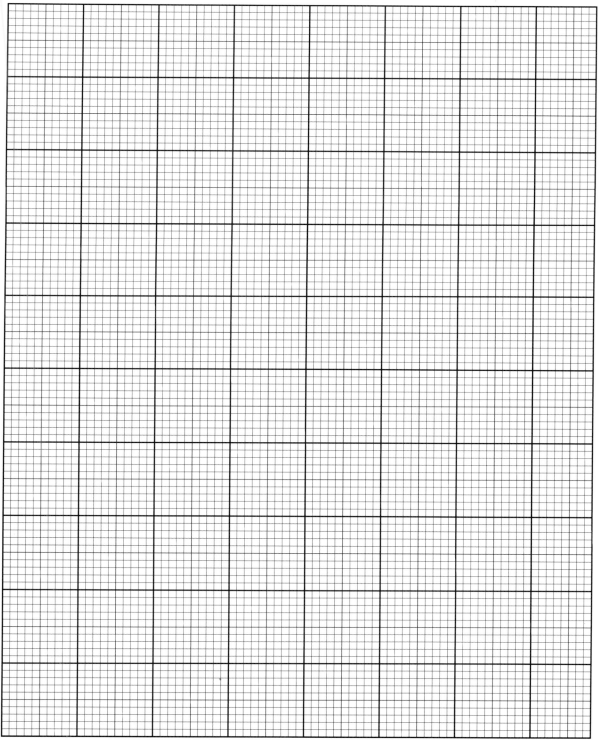

EACH LARGE SQUARE = 1M, EACH SMALL SQUARE = 10CM

NOTES

YOUR PLANS SCALE 1:50

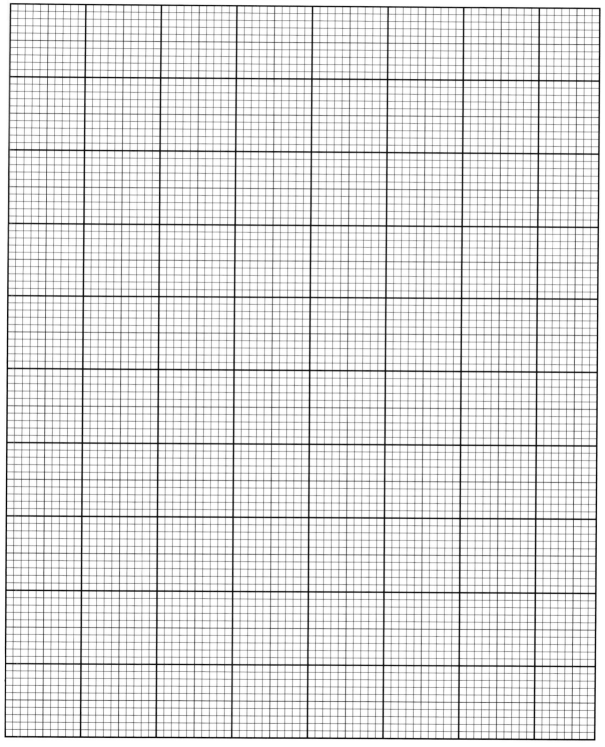

EACH LARGE SQUARE = 1M, EACH SMALL SQUARE = 10CM

NOTES

YOUR PLANS SCALE 1:25

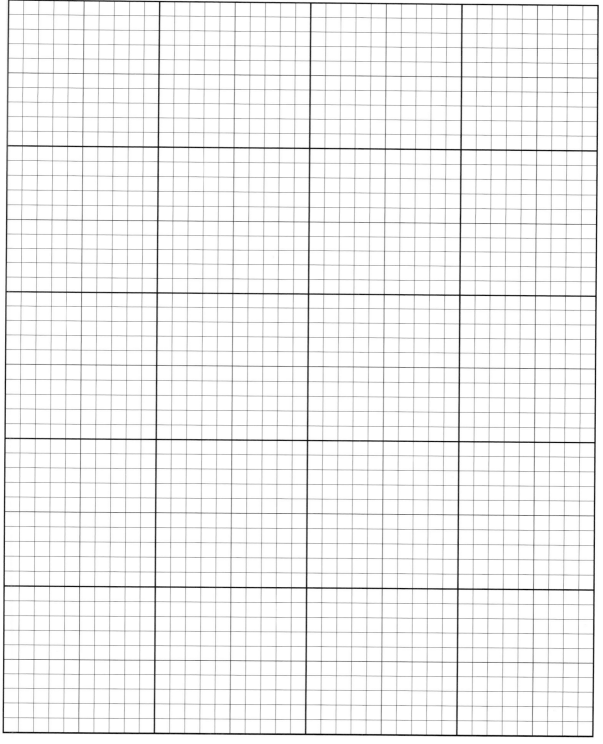

EACH LARGE SQUARE = 1M, EACH SMALL SQUARE = 10CM

NOTES

YOUR PLANS SCALE 1:25

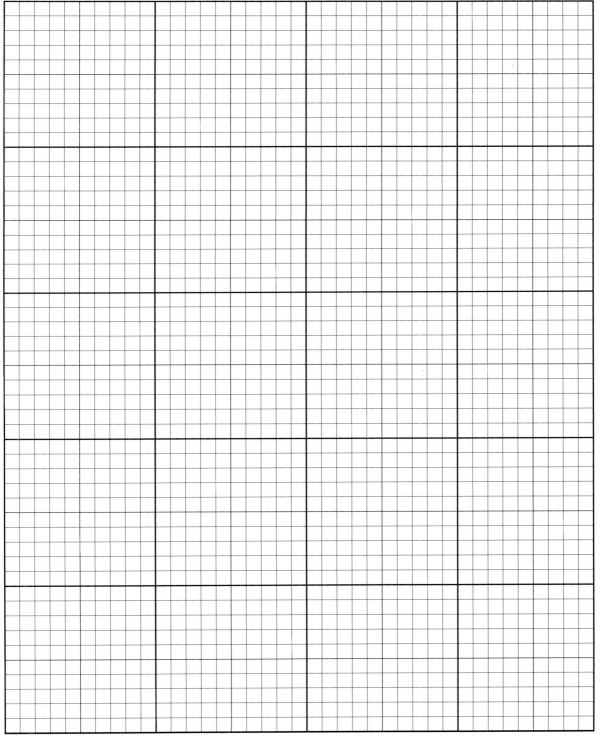

EACH LARGE SQUARE = 1M, EACH SMALL SQUARE = 10CM

NOTES